SELECTIONS FROM

The Book of Common Prayer

IN LARGE PRINT

The Church Hymnal Corporation
19 East 34th Street, New York, NY 10016

Certificate

I certify that the rites and prayers from The Book of Common Prayer, included in this edition, have been compared with the texts approved by the General Convention of 1979 as the Canons prescribe, and that they conform thereto.

Charles Mortimer Guilbert
Custodian of the Standard Book of Common Prayer
July, 1982

Copyright © 1982 by The Church Pension Fund
ISBN 0-89869-065-X

Contents

Preface

The liturgy of the Church reflects a concern for all its members. It is this care that has brought to production a large-print edition of selected parts of *The Book of Common Prayer.* This prayer book is designed to meet the needs of the visually impaired through the use of a special size of print, typeface, and using paper with a particular opacity. Recognizing the fact of multiple decrements a special binding and paper has been used to assist those people who experience the pain of arthritis and similar disorders.

This book is designed primarily for public worship, recognizing the members of our parishes who suffer from these physical handicaps and inviting them to full participation in the life of the Body of Christ. The book will welcome these people and will emphasize the totality of the Christian community and experience. It is hoped that this invitation will be made not only to persons who are visually handicapped but also to those suffering from other disabilities. Our Lord's ministry directly touched these people and they are an important sign of the life of Christ in the Body, and they need to be invited and included in its normal life of worship. In addition, this book includes material that can be used for private devotions to satisfy the increasing hunger for the life of prayer. Any prayer book is a meager instrument in developing a whole life of prayer, but it can be a useful tool and a sign of the Church's concern to some people.

This work is being cosponsored by the Episcopal Society for Ministry on Aging and The Church Hymnal Corporation. Grants for development and production were made by the Episcopal Church Foundation, The Bible and Common Prayer Book Society of the Episcopal Church and the office of Social and Specialized Ministries of the Executive Council. Grateful acknowledgement is made to the American Foundation for the Blind, The Library of Congress: Division for the Blind and Physically Handicapped and the National Society for the Prevention of Blindness for technical assistance.

The members of Grace Church, Colorado Springs, especially the members of the Committee on Aging have been of great support in this project. Our parish secretaries, Sally Hopkins and Thelma Brittain, did more than their duty. Imogene Merritt and Ethel Boatright have given special advice. The Committee on Aging at the Diocese of Colorado have been personally strengthening. Jennifer Stiefel's suggestions and sensitivity have contributed much. The art and design work of Nelson Gruppo and The Church Hymnal Corporation has made this more than a technical piece. Special thanks to The Reverend Canon Charles Mortimer Guilbert, whose insight, enthusiasm and direction have made this possible. There are many others unnamed who have helped in substantial and subtle ways, and to them we give our sincere thanks.

The Reverend E. William Pounds
Grace Church, Colorado Springs, Colorado
and Member of the Board of Directors,
The Episcopal Society for Ministry on Aging

Daily Morning Prayer: Rite One

Opening Sentences

Confession of Sin

The Officiant says to the people

Let us humbly confess our sins unto Almighty God.

Silence may be kept.

Officiant and People together, all kneeling

Almighty and most merciful Father, we have erred and strayed from thy ways like lost sheep, we have followed too much the devices and desires of our own hearts, we have offended against thy holy laws, we have left undone those things which we ought to have done, and we have done those things which we ought not to have done.

But thou, O Lord, have mercy upon us, spare thou those who confess their faults, restore thou those who are penitent, according to thy promises declared unto mankind in Christ Jesus our Lord; and grant, O most merciful Father, for his sake, that we may hereafter live a godly, righteous, and sober life, to the glory of thy holy Name. Amen.

The Priest alone stands and says

The Almighty and merciful Lord grant you absolution and remission of all your sins, true repentance, amendment of life, and the grace and consolation of his Holy Spirit. *Amen.*

The Invitatory and Psalter

Al/stand

Officiant O Lord, open thou our lips.
People And our mouth shall show forth thy praise.

Officiant and People

Glory to the Father, and to the Son, and to the Holy Spirit: as it was in the beginning, is now, and will be for ever. Amen.

Except in Lent, Alleluia *may be added.*

Then follows one of the Invitatory Psalms, Venite or Jubilate.

Venite

O come, let us sing unto the Lord; * let us heartily rejoice in the strength of our salvation. Let us come before his presence with thanksgiving, * and show ourselves glad in him with psalms.

For the Lord is a great God, * and a great King above all gods. In his hand are all the corners of the earth, * and the strength of the hills is his also. The sea is his and he made it, * and his hands prepared the dry land.

O come, let us worship and fall down * and kneel before the Lord our Maker. For he is the Lord our God,* and we are the people of his pasture and the sheep of his hand.

O worship the Lord in the beauty of holiness; * let the whole earth stand in awe of him. For he cometh, for he cometh to judge the earth, * and with righteousness to judge the world and the peoples with his truth.

Jubilate

O be joyful in the Lord all ye lands; * serve

the Lord with gladness and come before his presence with a song.

Be ye sure that the Lord he is God; it is he that hath made us and not we ourselves; * we are his people and the sheep of his pasture.

O go your way into his gates with thanksgiving and into his courts with praise; * be thankful unto him and speak good of his Name.

For the Lord is gracious; his mercy is everlasting;* and his truth endureth from generation to generation.

Christ our Passover

Alleluia. Christ our Passover is sacrificed for us, * therefore let us keep the feast, not with old leaven, neither with the leaven of malice and wickedness, * but with the unleavened bread of sincerity and truth. Alleluia.

Christ being raised from the dead-dieth no more; * death hath no more dominion over him. For in that he died, he died unto sin once; * but in that he liveth, he liveth unto God. Likewise reckon ye also yourselves to be dead indeed unto sin, * but alive unto God through Jesus Christ our Lord. Alleluia.

Christ is risen from the dead, * and become the first fruits of them_ that slept. For since by man came death, * by man came also the resurrection of the dead. For as in Adam all die, * even so in Christ shall all be made alive. Alleluia.

Then follows

The Psalm or Psalms Appointed

At the end of the Psalms is sung or said

Glory to the Father, and to the Son, and to the Holy Spirit: as it was in the beginning, is now, and will be for ever. Amen.

The Lessons

One or two Lessons, as appointed, are read, the Reader. first saying

A Reading (Lesson) from ____________.

After each Lesson the Reader may say

The Word of the Lord.

Answer Thanks be to God.

Silence may be kept after each Reading. One of the following Canticles, is sung or said after each Reading.

1 A Song of Creation

I *Invocation*

O all ye works of the Lord, bless ye the Lord;
* praise him and magnify him for ever. O ye angels of the Lord, bless ye the Lord;* praise him and magnify him for ever.

II *The Cosmic Order*

O ye heavens, bless ye the Lord; * O ye waters that be above the firmament, bless ye the Lord; O all ye powers of the Lord, bless ye the Lord; * praise ·him and magnify him for ever.

O ye sun and moon, bless ye the Lord;* O ye stars of heaven, bless ye the Lord; O ye showers and dew, bless ye the Lord; * praise him and magnify him for ever.

O ye winds of God, bless ye the Lord; * O ye fire and heat, bless ye the Lord; O ye winter and summer, bless ye the Lord; * praise him and magnify him for ever.

O ye dews and frosts, bless ye the Lord;* O ye frost and cold, bless ye the Lord; O ye ice and snow, bless ye the Lord; * praise him and magnify him for ever.

O ye nights and days, bless ye the Lord; * O

ye light and darkness, bless ye the Lord; O ye lightnings and clouds, bless ye the Lord; * praise him and magnify him for ever.

III *The Earth and its Creatures*

O let the earth bless the Lord; * O ye mountains and hills, bless ye the Lord; O all ye gre'en things upon the earth, bless ye the Lord; * praise him and magnify him for ever.

O ye wells, bless ye the Lord; * O ye seas and floods, bless ye the Lord; O ye whales and all that move in the waters, bless ye the Lord; praise him and magnify him for ever.

O all ye fowls of the air, bless ye the Lord;* O all ye beasts and cattle, bless ye the Lord; O ye children of men, bless ye the Lord; * praise him and magnify him for ever.

IV *The People of God*

O ye people of God, bless ye the Lord; * O ye

priests of the Lord, bless ye the Lord; O ye servants of the Lord, bless ye the Lord; * praise him and magnify him for ever.

O ye spirits and souls of the righteous, bless ye the Lord; * O ye holy and humble men of heart, bless ye the Lord. Let us bless the Fa- ther, the Son, and the Holy Spirit;* praise him and magnify him for ever.

2 A Song of Praise

Blessed art thou, O Lord God of our fathers;* praised and exalted above all for ever. Blessed art thou for the Name of thy Majesty; * praised and exalted above all for ever. Blessed art thou in the temple of thy holiness; * praised and exalted above all for ever. Blessed art thou that beholdest the depths, and dwellest between the Cherubim; * praised and exalted above all for ever. Blessed art thou on the glorious throne of thy kingdom; * praised and exalted above all for ever. Blessed art thou in the firmament of heaven; * praised and exalted above all for ever. Blessed art thou, O Father, Son, and Holy Spirit;* praised and exalted above all for ever.

3 The Song of Mary

My soul doth magnify the Lord, * and my spirit hath rejoiced in God my Savior. For he hath regarded * the lowliness of his handmaiden. For behold from henceforth * all generations shall call me blessed. For he that is mighty hath magnified me, * and holy is his Name. And his mercy is on them that fear him * throughout all generations. He hath showed strength with his arm; * he hath scattered the proud in the imagination of their hearts. He hath put down the mighty from their seat, * and hath exalted the humble and meek. He hath filled the hungry with good things, * and the rich he hath sent empty away. He remembering his mercy hath holpen his servant Israel, * as he promised to our forefathers, Abraham and his seed for ever.

Glory to the Father, and to the Son, and to the Holy Spirit: * as it was in the beginning, is now, and will be for ever. Amen.

4 The Song of Zechariah

Blessed be the Lord God of Israel, * for he hath visited and redeemed his people; and hath raised up a mighty salvation for us* in the house of his servant David, as he spake by the mouth of his holy prophets, * which have been since the world began:

That we should be saved from our enemies, * and from the hand of all that hate us; to perform the mercy promised to our forefathers, * and to remember his holy covenant; to perform the oath which he sware to our fore-father Abraham, * that he would give us, that we being delivered out of the hand of our ene-mies * might serve him without fear, in holi-ness and righteousness before him, * all the days of our life.

And thou, child, shalt be called the prophet of the Highest, * for thou shalt go before the face of the Lord to prepare his ways; to give knowledge of salvation unto his people * for the remission of their sins, through the tender mercy of our God, * whereby the dayspring from on high hath visited us; to give light to them that sit in darkness and in the shadow of death, * and to guide our feet into the way of peace.

Glory to the Father, and to the Son, and to the Holy Spirit: * as it was in the beginning, is now, and will be for ever. Amen.

5 The Song of Simeon

Lord, now lettest thou thy servant depart in peace,* according to thy word; for mine eyes have seen thy salvation, * which thou hast prepared before the face of all people, to be a light to lighten the Gentiles, * and to be the glory of thy people Israel.

Glory to the Father, and to the Son, and to the Holy Spirit: * as it was in the beginning, is now, and will be for ever. Amen.

6 Glory be to God

Glory be to God on high, and on earth peace, good will towards men.

We praise thee, we bless thee, we worship thee, we glorify thee, we give thanks to thee for thy great glory, O Lord God, heavenly King, God the Father Almighty.

O Lord, the only-begotten Son, Jesus Christ; O Lord God, Lamb of God, Son of the Father, that takest away the sins of the world, have mercy upon us. Thou that takest away the sins of the world, receive our prayer. Thou that sittest at the right hand of God the Father, have mercy upon us.

For thou only art holy, thou only art the Lord, thou only, O Christ, with the Holy Ghost, art most high in the glory of God the Father. Amen.

7 We Praise Thee

We praise thee, O God; we acknowledge thee to be the Lord. All the earth doth worship thee, the Father everlasting. To thee all Angels cry aloud, the Heavens and all the Powers therein. To thee Cherubim and Seraphim continually do cry:

Holy, holy, holy, Lord God of Sabaoth; Heaven and earth are full of the majesty of thy glory, The glorious company of the apostles praise thee. The goodly fellowship of the prophets praise thee. The noble army of martyrs praise thee. The holy Church throughout all the world doth acknowledge thee, the Father, of an infinite majesty, thine adorable, true, and only Son, also the Holy Ghost the Comforter.

Thou art the King of glory, O Christ. Thou art the everlasting Son of the Father. When thou tookest upon thee to deliver man, thou didst humble thyself to be born of a Virgin. When thou hadst overcome the sharpness of death, thou didst open the kingdom of heaven to all believers. Thou sittest at the right hand of God, in the glory of the Father. We believe that thou shalt come to be our judge. We therefore pray thee, help thy servants, whom thou hast redeemed with thy precious blood.

Make them to be numbered with thy saints, in glory everlasting.

The Apostles' Creed

Officiant and People together, all standing

I believe in God, the Father almighty, maker of heaven and earth; and in Jesus Christ his only Son our Lord; who was conceived by the Holy Ghost, born of the Virgin Mary, suffered under Pontius Pilate, was crucified, dead, and buried. He descended into hell.

The third day he rose again from the dead. He ascended into heaven, and sitteth on the right hand of God the Father almighty. From thence he shall come to judge the -quick and the de-ad. I believe in the Holy Ghost, the holy catholic Church, the communion of saints, the forgiveness of sins, the resurrection of the body, and the life everlasting. Amen.

The Prayers

The people stand or kneel

Officiant The Lord be with you.

People And with thy spirit.

Officiant Let us pray.

Officiant and People

Our Father, who art in heaven, hallowed be thy Name, thy kingdom come, thy will be done, on earth as it is in heaven. Give us this day our daily bread. And forgive us our trespasses, as we forgive those who trespass against us. And lead us not into temptation, but deliver us from evil. For thine is the kingdom, and the power, and the glory, for ever and ever. Amen.

Then follows one of the following sets of Suffrages

A

V. O Lord, show thy mercy upon us;

R. And grant us thy salvation.

V. Endue thy ministers with righteousness;

R. And make thy chosen people joyful.

V. Give peace, O Lord, in all the world;

R. For only in thee can we live in safety.

V. Lord, keep this nation under thy care;

R. And guide us in the way of justice and truth.

V. Let thy way be known upon earth;

R. Thy saving health among all nations.

V. Let not the needy, O Lord, be forgotten;

R. Nor the hope of the poor be taken away.

V. Create in us clean hearts, O God;

R. And sustain us with thy Holy Spirit.

B

V. O Lord, save thy people, and bless thine heritage;

R. Govern them and lift them up for ever.

V. Day by day we magnify thee;

R. And we worship thy Name ever, world without end.

V. Vouchsafe, O Lord, to keep us this day without sin;

R. O Lord, have mercy upon us, have mercy upon us.

V. O Lord, let thy mercy be upon us;

R. As our trust is in thee.

V. O Lord, in thee have I trusted;

R. Let me never be confounded.

The Collect of the Day

A Collect for Sundays

O God, who makest us glad with the weekly remembrance of the glorious resurrection of thy Son our Lord: Grant us this day such blessing through our worship of thee, that the days to come may be spent in thy favor; through the same Jesus Christ our Lord. *Amen.*

A Collect for Fridays

Almighty God, whose most dear Son went not up to joy but first he suffered pain, and entered not into glory before he was crucified: Mercifully grant that we, walking in the way of the cross, may find it none other than the way of life and peace; through the same thy Son Jesus Christ our Lord. *Amen.*

A Collect for Saturdays

Almighty God, who after the creation of the world didst rest from all thy works and sanctify a day of rest for all thy creatures: Grant that we, putting away all earthly anxieties, may be duly prepared for the service of thy sanctuary, and that our rest here upon earth may be a preparation for the eternal rest promised to thy people in heaven; through Jesus Christ our Lord. *Amen.*

A Collect for the Renewal of Life

O God, the King eternal, who dividest the day from the night and turnest the shadow of death into the morning: Drive far from us all wrong desires, incline our hearts to keep thy law, and guide our feet into the way of peace; that, having done thy will with cheerfulness while it was day, we may, when the night cometh, rejoice to give thee thanks; through Jesus Christ our Lord. *Amen.*

A Collect for Peace

O God, who art the author of peace and lover of concord, in knowledge of whom standeth our eternal life, whose service is perfect freedom: Defend us, thy humble servants, in all assaults of our enemies; that we, surely trusting in thy defense, may not fear the power of any adversaries; through the might of Jesus Christ our Lord. *Amen.*

A Collect for Grace

O Lord, our heavenly Father, almighty and everlasting God, who hast safely brought us to the beginning of this day: Defend us in the same with thy mighty power; and grant that this day we fall into no sin, neither run into any kind of danger; but that we, being ordered by thy governance, may do always what is righteous in thy sight; through Jesus Christ our Lord. *Amen.*

A Collect for Guidance

O heavenly Father, in whom we live and move and have our being: We humbly pray thee so to guide and govern us by thy Holy Spirit, that in all the cares and occupations of our life we may not forget thee, but may remember that we are ever walking in thy sight; through Jesus Christ our Lord. *Amen.*

The Collects for Mission

Almighty and everlasting God, by whose Spirit the whole body of thy faithful people is governed and sanctified: Receive our supplications and prayers which we offer before thee for all members of thy holy Church, that in their vocation and ministry they may truly and godly serve thee; through our Lord and Savior Jesus Christ. *Amen.*

or this

O God, who hast made of one blood all the peoples of the earth, and didst send thy blessed Son to preach peace to those who are far off and to those who are near: Grant that people everywhere may seek after thee and find thee; bring the nations into thy fold; pour out thy Spirit upon all flesh; and hasten the coming of thy kingdom; through the same thy Son Jesus Christ our Lord. *Amen.*

or the following

Lord Jesus Christ, who didst stretch out thine arms of love on the hard wood of the cross that everyone might come within the reach of thy saving embrace: So clothe us in thy Spirit that we, reaching forth our hands in love, may bring those who do not know thee to the knowledge and love of thee; for the honor of thy Name. *Amen.*

Here may be sung a hymn or anthem.

Authorized intercessions and thanksgivings may follow.

The General Thanksgiving

Officiant and People

Almighty God, Father of all mercies, we thine unworthy servants do give thee most humble and hearty thanks for all thy goodness and loving-kindness to us and to all men. We bless thee for our creation, preservation, and all the blessings of this life; but above all for thine inestimable love in the redemption of the world by our Lord Jesus Christ, for the means of grace, and for the hope of glory. And, we beseech thee, give us that due sense of all thy mercies, that our hearts may be unfeignedly thankful; and that we show forth thy praise, not only with our lips, but in our lives, by giving up our selves to thy service, and by walking before thee in holiness and righteousness all our days; through Jesus Christ our Lord, to whom, with thee and the Holy Ghost, be all honor and glory, world without end. *Amen.*

A Prayer of St. Chrysostom

Almighty God, who hast given us grace at this time with one accord to make our common supplication unto thee, and hast promised through thy well-beloved Son that when two or three are gathered together in his Name thou wilt be in the midst of them: Fulfill now, O

Lord, the desires and petitions of thy servants as may be best for us; granting us in this world knowledge of thy truth, and in the world to come life everlasting. *Amen.*

Then may be said

Let us bless the Lord. *Thanks be to God.*

The Officiant may then conclude with one of the following

The grace of our Lord Jesus Christ, and the love of God, and the fellowship of the Holy Ghost, be with us all evermore. *Amen.*

May the God of hope fill us with all joy and peace in believing through the power of the Holy Spirit. *Amen.*

Glory to God whose power, working in us, can do infinitely more than we can ask or imagine: Glory to him from generation to generation in the Church, and in Christ Jesus for ever and ever. *Amen.*

Daily Devotions for Individuals and Families

In the Morning

From Psalm 51

Open my lips, O Lord, * and my mouth shall proclaim your praise. Create in me a clean heart, O God,* and renew a right spirit within me. Cast me not away from your presence * and take not your holy Spirit from me. Give me the joy of your saving help again * and sustain me with your bountiful Spirit. Glory to the Father, and to the Son, and to the Holy Spirit: * as it was in the beginning, is now, and will be for ever. *Amen.*

A Reading

Blessed be the God and Father of our Lord Jesus Christ! By his great mercy we have been born anew to a living hope through the resurrection of Jesus Christ from the dead.
1 Peter 1:3

Other readings and recordings may be used at this time; the Apostles' Creed may be said and prayers may be offered for ourselves and others.

The Lord's Prayer

The Collect

Lord God, almighty and everlasting Father, you have brought us in safety to this new day: Preserve us with your mighty power, that we may not fall into sin, nor be overcome by adversity; and in all we do, direct us to the fulfilling of your purpose; through Jesus Christ our Lord. *Amen.*

At Noon

From Psalm 113

Give praise, you servants of the LORD; * praise the Name of the LORD. Let the Name of the LORD be blessed,* from this time forth for evermore. From the rising of the sun to its going down * let the Name of the LORD be praised. The LORD is high above all nations, * and his glory above the heavens.

A Reading

O God, you will keep in perfect peace those whose minds are fixed on you; for in returning and rest we shall be saved; in quietness and trust shall be our strength. *Isaiah 26:3; 30:15*

Prayers may be offered for ourselves and others.

The Lord's Prayer

The Collect

Blessed Savior, at this hour you hung upon the cross, stretching out your loving arms: Grant that all the peoples of the earth may look to you and be saved; for your mercies' sake. *Amen.*

or this

Lord Jesus Christ, you said to your apostles, "Peace I give to you; my own peace I leave with you": Regard not our sins, but the faith of your Church, and give to us the peace and unity of that heavenly City, where with the Father and the Holy Spirit you live and reign, now and for ever. *Amen.*

In the Early Evening

This devotion may be used before or after the evening meal.

O gracious Light, pure brightness of the everliving Father in heaven, O Jesus Christ, holy and blessed!

Now as we come to the setting of the sun, and our eyes behold the vesper light, we sing your praises O God: Father, Son, and Holy Spirit.

You are worthy at all times to be praised by happy voices, O Son of God, O Giver of life, and to be glorified through all the worlds.

A Reading

It is not ourselves that we proclaim; we proclaim Christ Jesus as Lord, and ourselves as your servants, for Jesus' sake. For the same God who said, "Out of darkness let light shine," has caused his light to shine within us, to give the light of revelation-the revelation of the glory of God in the face of Jesus Christ. *2 Corinthians 4:5-6*

Prayers may be offered for ourselves and others.

The Lord's Prayer

The Collect

Lord Jesus, stay with us, for evening is at hand and the day is past; be our companion in the way, kindle our hearts, and awaken hope, that we may know you as you are revealed in Scripture and the breaking of bread. Grant this for the sake of your love. *Amen.*

At the Close of Day

Psalm 134

Behold now, bless the LORD, all you servants of the LORD, * you that stand by night in the house of the LORD. Lift up your hands in the holy place and bless the LORD; * the LORD who made heaven and earth bless you out of Zion.

A Reading

Lord, you are in the midst of us and we are called by your Name: Do not forsake us, O Lord our God. *Jeremiah 14:9,22*

The following may be said

Lord, you now have set your servant free* to go in peace as you have promised; for these eyes of mine have seen the Savior, * whom you have prepared for all the world to see: a Light to enlighten the nations, * and the glory of your people Israel.

Other readings and recordings may be used at this time; the Apostles' creed may be said and prayers may be offered for ourselves and others. Prayers of thanksgiving for the blessings of the day, and penitence for our sins may be included.

The Lord's Prayer

The Collect

Visit this place, O Lord, and drive far from it all snares of the enemy; let your holy angels dwell with us to preserve us in peace; and let your blessing be upon us always; through Jesus Christ our Lord. *Amen.*

The almighty and merciful Lord, Father, Son, and Holy Spirit, bless us and keep us. *Amen.*

Holy Baptism

A hymn, psalm, or anthem may be sung.

The people standing, the Celebrant says

Blessed be God: Father, Son, and Holy Spirit.

People And blessed be his kingdom, now and for ever. Amen.

In place of the above, from Easter Day through the Day of Pentecost

Celebrant Alleluia. Christ is risen.
People The Lord is risen indeed. Alleluia.

In Lent and on other penitential occasions

Celebrant Bless the Lord who forgives all our sins;

People His mercy endures for ever.

The Celebrant then continues

There is one Body and one Spirit;

People There is one hope in God's call to us,

Celebrant One Lord, one Faith, one Baptism;

People One God and Father of all.

Celebrant The Lord be with you.

People And also with you.

Celebrant Let us pray.

The Collect of the Day

People Amen.

The Lessons

The people sit. One or two Lessons, as appointed, are read, the Reader first saying

A Reading (Lesson) from __________

After each Reading, the Reader may say

The Word of the Lord.

People Thanks be to God.

Silence may follow.

A Psalm, hymn, or anthem may follow each Reading.

Then, all standing, the Deacon or a Priest reads the Gospel, first saying

The Holy Gospel of our Lord Jesus Christ according to __________

People Glory to you, Lord Christ.

After the Gospel, the Reader says

The Gospel of the Lord.

People Praise to you, Lord Christ.

The Sermon

Or the Sermon may be preached after the Peace.

Presentation and Examination of the Candidates

The Celebrant says

The Candidate(s) for Holy Baptism will now be presented.

Adults and Older Children

The candidates who are able to answer for themselves are presented individually by their Sponsors, as follows

Sponsor I present *N.* to receive the Sacrament of Baptism.

The Celebrant asks each candidate when presented

Do you desire to be baptized?

Candidate I do.

Infants and Younger Children

Then the candidates unable to answer for themselves are presented individually by their Parents and Godparents, as follows

Parents and Godparents

I present *N.* to receive the Sacrament of Baptism.

When all have been presented the Celebrant asks the parents and godparents

Will you be responsible for seeing that the child you present is brought up in the Christian faith and life?

Parents and Godparents

I will, with God's help.

Celebrant

Will you by your prayers and witness help this child to grow into the full stature of Christ?

Parents and Godparents

I will, with God's help.

Then the Celebrant asks the following questions of the candidates who can speak for themselves, and of the parents and godparents who speak on be- half of the infants and younger children

Question Do you renounce Satan and all the spiritual forces of wickedness that rebel against God?

Answer I renounce them.

Question Do you renounce the evil powers of this world which corrupt and destroy the creatures of God?

Answer I renounce them.

Question Do you renounce all sinful desires that draw you from the love of God?

Answer I renounce them.

Question Do you turn to Jesus Christ and accept him as your Savior?

Answer Ida.

Question Do you put your whole trust in his grace and love?

Answer Ida.

Question Do you promise to follow and obey him as your Lord?

Answer Ida.

Others may be presented and examined.

After alt have been presented, the Celebrant addresses the congregation, saying

Will you who witness these vows do all in

your power to support *these persons* in *their* life in Christ?

People We will.

The Celebrant then says these. or similar words

Let us join with *those* who *are* committing *themselves* to Christ and renew our own baptismal covenant.

The Baptismal Covenant

Celebrant Do you believe in God the Father?

People I believe in God, the Father almighty, creator of heaven and earth.

Celebrant Do you believe in Jesus Christ, the Son of God?

People I believe in Jesus Christ, his only Son, our Lord. He was conceived by the power of the Holy Spirit and born of the Virgin Mary. He suffered under Pontius Pilate, was crucified, died, and was buried. He descended to the dead. On the third day he rose again. He ascended into heaven, and is seated at the right hand of the Father. He will come again to judge the living and the dead.

Celebrant Do you believe in God the Holy Spirit?

People I believe in the Holy Spirit, the holy catholic Church, the communion of saints, the forgiveness of sins, the resurrection of the body, and the life everlasting.

Celebrant Will you continue in the apostles' teaching and fellowship, in the breaking of bread, and 1n the prayers?

People I will, with God's help.

Celebrant Will you persevere in resisting evil, and, whenever you fall into sin, repent and return to the Lord?

People I will, with God's help.

Celebrant Will you proclaim by word and example the Good News of God in Christ?

People I will, with God's help.

Celebrant Will you seek and serve Christ in all persons, loving your neighbor as yourself?

People I will, with God's help.

Celebrant Will you strive for justice and peace among all people, and respect the dignity of every human being?

People I will, with God's help.

Prayers for the Candidates

Tho Colcbrant then says to the congregation

Let us now pray for *these persons* who *are* to receive the Sacrament of new birth [and for those (this person) who *have* renewed *their* commitment to Christ.]

A Person appointed leads the following petitions

Leader Deliver *them, O* Lord, from the way of sin and death.

People Lord, hear our prayer.

Leader Open *their hearts* to your grace and truth.

People Lord, hear our prayer.

Leader Fill *them* with your holy and life-giving Spirit.

People Lord, hear our prayer.

Leader Keep *them* in the faith and communion of your holy Church.

People Lord, hear our prayer.

Leader Teach *them* to love others in the power of the Spirit.

People Lord, hear our prayer.

Leader Send *them* into the world in witness to your love.

People Lord, hear our prayer.

Leader Bring *them* to the fullness of your peace and glory.

People Lord, hear our prayer.

The Celebrant says

Grant, O Lord, that all who are baptized into the death of Jesus Christ your Son may live in the power of his resurrection and look for him to come again in glory; who lives and reigns now and for ever. *Amen.*

Thanksgiving over the Water

The Celebrant blesses the water, first saying

The Lord be with you.

People And also with you.

Celebrant Let us give thanks to the Lord our God.

People It is right to give him thanks and praise.

Celebrant

We thank you, Almighty God, for the gift of water. Over it the Holy Spirit moved in the beginning of creation. Through it you led the children of Israel out of their bondage in Egypt into the land of promise. In it your son Jesus received the baptism of John and was anointed by the Holy Spirit as the Messiah, the Christ, to lead us, through his death and resurrection, from the bondage of sin into everlasting life.

We thank you, Father, for the water of Baptism. In it we are buried with Christ in his death. By it we share in his resurrection. Through it we are reborn by the Holy Spirit. Therefore in joyful obedience to your Son, we bring into his fellowship those who come to him in faith, baptizing them in the Name of the Father, and of the Son, and of the Holy Spirit.

At the following words, the Celebrant touches the water

Now sanctify this water, we pray you, by the power of your Holy Spirit, that those who here are cleansed from sin and born again may continue for ever in the risen life of Jesus Christ our Savior.

To him, to you, and to the Holy Spirit, be all honor and glory, now and for ever. *Amen.*

The Bishop may then consecrate oil of Chrism.

The Baptism

Each candidate is presented by name to the Celebrant, or to an assisting priest or deacon, who then immerses, or pours water upon, the candidate, saying

N., I baptize you in the Name of the Father, and of the Son, and of the Holy Spirit. *Amen.*

When this action has been completed for all candidates, the Bishop or Priest, at a place in full sight of the congregation, prays over them, saying

Let us pray.

Heavenly Father, we thank you that by water and the Holy Spirit you have bestowed upon *these* your *servants* the forgiveness of sin, and have raised *them* to the new life of grace. Sustain *them,* O Lord, in your Holy Spirit. Give *them* an inquiring and discerning heart, the courage to will and to persevere, a spirit to know and to love you, and the gift of joy and wonder in all your works. *Amen.*

N., you are sealed by the Holy Spirit in Baptism and marked as Christ's own for ever. *Amen.*

When all have been baptized, the Celebrant says

Let us welcome the newly baptized.

Celebrant and People

We receive you into the household of God. Confess the faith of Christ crucified, proclaim his resurrection, and share with us in his eternal priesthood.

If Confirmation, Reception, or the Reaffirmation of Baptismal Vows is not to follow, the Peace is now exchanged

Celebrant The peace of the Lord be always with you.

People And also with you.

A Penitential Order: Rite One

For use at the beginning of the Liturgy, or as a separate service.

A hymn, psalm, or anthem may be sung.

The people standing, the Celebrant says

Blessed be God: Father, Son, and Holy Spirit.

People And blessed be his kingdom, now and for ever. Amen.

In place of the above, from Easter Day through the Day of Pentecost

Celebrant Alleluia. Christ is risen.
People The Lord is risen indeed. Alleluia.

In Lent and on other penitential occasions

Celebrant Bless the Lord who forgiveth all our sins;

People His mercy endureth for ever.

The Decalogue may be said, the people kneeling.

The Celebrant may read one of the following sentences

Hear what our Lord Jesus Christ saith: Thou shalt love the Lord thy God with all thy heart, and with all thy soul, and with all thy mind. This is the first and great commandment. And the second is like unto it: Thou shalt love thy neighbor as thyself. On these two commandments hang all the Law and the Prophets. *Matthew 22:37-40*

If we say that we have no sin, we deceive ourselves, and the truth is not in us; but if we confess our sins, God is faithful and just to forgive us our sins, and to cleanse us from all unrighteousness. *I John 1:8,* 9

Seeing that we have a great high priest, that is passed into the heavens, Jesus the Son of

God, let us come boldly unto the throne of grace, that we may obtain mercy, and find grace to help in time of need. *Hebrews 4:14, 16*

The Deacon or Celebrant then says

Let us humbly confess our sins unto Almighty God.

Silence may be kept.

Minister and People

Most merciful God, we confess that we have sinned against thee in thought, word, and deed, by what we have done, and by what we have left undone. We have not loved thee with our whole heart; we have not loved our neighbors as ourselves. We are truly sorry and we humbly repent. For the sake of thy Son Jesus Christ, have mercy on us and forgive us; that we may delight in thy will, and walk in thy ways, to the glory of thy Name. Amen.

The Bishop when present, or the Priest, stands and says

The Almighty and merciful Lord grant you absolution and remission of all your sins, true repentance, amendment of life, and the grace and consolation of his Holy Spirit. *Amen.*

When this Order is used at the beginning of the Liturgy, the service continues with the Kyrie eleison, the Trisagion, or the Gloria in excelsis.

When used separately, it concludes with suitable prayers, and the Grace or a blessing.

The Holy Eucharist: Rite One

The Word of God

A hymn, psalm, or anthem may be sung.

The people standing, the Celebrant may say

Blessed be God: Father, Son, and Holy Spirit.

People And blessed be his kingdom, now and for ever. Amen.

In place of the above, from Easter Day through the Day of Pentecost

Celebrant Alleluia. Christ is risen.

People The Lord is risen indeed. Alleluia.

In Lent and on other penitential occasions

Celebrant Bless the Lord who forgiveth all our sins;

People His mercy endureth for ever.

The Celebrant says

Almighty God, unto whom all hearts are open, all desires known, and from whom no secrets are hid: Cleanse the thoughts of our hearts by the inspiration of thy Holy Spirit, that we may perfectly love thee, and worthily magnify thy holy Name; through Christ our Lord. *Amen.*

Then the Ten Commandments may be said, or the following

Hear what our Lord Jesus Christ saith: Thou shalt love the Lord thy God with all thy heart, and with all thy soul, and with all thy mind. This is the first and great commandment. And the second is like unto it: Thou shalt love thy neighbor as thyself. On these two commandments hang all the Law and the Prophets.

Here is sung or said

Lord, have mercy upon us. *Christ, have mercy upon us.* Lord, have mercy upon us.

or this

Kyrie eleison. *Christe eleison.* Kyrie eleison.

or this

Holy God, Holy and Mighty, Holy Immortal One, *Have mercy upon us.*

When appointed, the following hymn or some other song of praise is sung or said, in addition to, or in place of, the preceding, all standing

Glory be to God on high, and on earth peace, good will towards men.

We praise thee, we bless thee, we worship thee, we glorify thee, we give thanks to thee for thy great glory, O Lord God, heavenly King, God the Father Almighty.

O Lord, the only-begotten son, Jesus Christ; O Lord God, Lamb of God, Son of the Father, that takest away the sins of the world, have mercy upon us. Thou that takest away the sins of the world, receive our prayer. Thou that sittest at the right hand of God the Father, have mercy upon us.

For thou only art holy; thou only art the Lord; thou only, O Christ, with the Holy Ghost, art most high in the glory of God the Father. Amen.

The Collect of the Day

The Celebrant says to the people

The Lord be with you.

People And with thy spirit.

Celebrant Let us pray.

The Celebrant says the Collect.

People Amen.

The Lessons

The people sit. One or two Lessons, as appointed, are read, the Reader first saying

A Reading (Lesson) from ________

After each Reading, the Reader may say

The Word of the Lord.

People Thanks be to God.

Silence may follow.

A Psalm, hymn, or anthem may follow each Reading.

Then, all standing, the Deacon or a Priest reads the Gospel, first saying

The Holy Gospel of our Lord Jesus Christ according to ____________

People Glory be to thee, O Lord.

After the Gospel the Reader says

The Go pel of the Lord.

People Praise be to thee, O Christ.

The Sermon

On Sundays and other Major Feasts there follows, all standing

The Nicene Creed

We believe in one God, the Father, the Almighty, maker of heaven and earth, of all that is, seen and unseen.

We believe in one Lord, Jesus Christ, the only Son of God, eternally begotten of the Father, God from God, Light from Light, true God from true God, begotten, not made, of one Being with the Father. Through him all things were made. For us and for our salvation he came down from heaven: by the power of the Holy Spirit he became incarnate from the Virgin Mary, and was made man. For our sake he was crucified under Pontius Pilate; he suffered death and was buried. On the third day he rose again in accordance with the Scriptures; he ascended into heaven and is seated at the right hand of the Father. He will come again in glory to judge the living and the dead, and his kingdom will have no end.

We believe in the Holy Spirit, the Lord, the giver of life, who proceeds from the Father and the Son. With the Father and the Son he is worshiped and glorified He has spoken through the Prophets. We believe in one holy catholic and apostolic Church. We acknowledge one baptism for the forgiveness of sins. We look for the resurrection of the dead, and the life of the world to come. Amen.

The Prayers of the People

Intercession is offered in the following form, or other authorized prayers.

The Deacon or other person appointed says

Let us pray for the whole state of Christ's Church and the world.

Almighty and everliving God, who in thy holy Word hast taught us to make prayers, and supplications, and to give thanks for all men: Receive these our prayers which we offer unto thy divine Majesty, beseeching thee to inspire continually the Universal Church with the spirit of truth, unity, and concord; and grant that all those who do confess thy holy

Name may agree in the truth of thy holy Word, and live in unity and godly love.

Give grace, O heavenly Father, to all bishops and other ministers [especially __________], that they may, both by their life and doctrine, set forth thy true and lively Word, and rightly and duly administer thy holy Sacraments.

And to all thy people give thy heavenly grace, and especially to this congregation here present; that, with meek heart and due reverence, they may hear and receive thy holy Word, truly serving thee in holiness and righteousness all the days of their life.

We beseech thee also so to rule the hearts of those who bear the authority of government in this and every land [especially __________], that they may be led to wise decisions and right actions for the welfare and peace of the world.

Open, O Lord, the eyes of all people to behold thy gracious hand in all thy works, that, rejoicing in thy whole creation, they may honor thee with their substance, and be faithful stewards of thy bounty.

And we most humbly beseech thee, of thy goodness, O Lord, to comfort and succor [__________ and] all those who, in this transitory life, are in trouble, sorrow, need, sickness, or any other adversity.

Additional petitions and thanksgivings may be included here.

And we also bless thy holy Name for all thy servants departed this life in thy faith and fear [especially __________], beseeching thee to grant them continual growth in thy love and service; and to grant us grace so to follow the good examples of [__________ and of] all thy saints, that with them we may be partakers of thy heavenly kingdom.

Grant these our prayers, O Father, for Jesus Christ's sake, our only Mediator and Advocate. *Amen.*

Confession of Sin

A Confession of Sin is said here if it has not been said earlier. On occasion, the Confession may be omitted. The Deacon or Celebrant says

Ye who do truly and earnestly repent you of your sins, and are in love and charity with your neighbors, and intend to lead a new life, following the commandments of God, and walking from henceforth in his holy ways: Draw near with faith, and make your humble confession to Almighty God, devoutly kneeling.

or this

Let us humbly confess our sins unto Almighty God.

Silence may be kept.

Minister and People

Almighty God, Father of our Lord Jesus Christ, maker of all things, judge of all men: We acknowledge and bewail our manifold sins and wickedness, which we from time to time most grievously have committed, by thought, word, and deed, against thy divine Majesty, provoking most justly thy wrath and indignation against us. We do earnestly repent, and are heartily sorry for these our misdoings; the remembrance of them is grievous unto us, the burden of them is intolerable. Have mercy upon us, have mercy upon us, most merciful Father; for thy Son our Lord Jesus Christ's sake, forgive us all that is past; and grant that we may ever hereafter serve and please thee in newness of life, to the honor and glory of thy Name; through Jesus Christ our Lord. Amen.

or the following

Most merciful God, we confess that we have sinned against thee in thought, word, and deed, by what we have done, and by what we have left undone. We have not loved thee with our whole heart; we have not loved our neighbors as ourselves. We are truly sorry and we humbly repent. For the sake of thy Son Jesus Christ, have mercy on us and forgive us; that we may delight in thy will, and walk in thy ways, to the glory of thy Name. Amen.

The Bishop when present, or the Priest, stands and says

Almighty God, our heavenly Father, who of his great mercy hath promised forgiveness of sins to all those who with hearty repentance and true faith turn unto him, have mercy upon you, pardon and deliver you from all your sins, confirm and strengthen you in all goodness, and bring you to everlasting life; through Jesus Christ our Lord. Amen.

A Minister may then say one or more of the following sentences, first saying

Hear the Word of God to all who truly turn to him.

Come unto me, all ye that travail and are heavy laden, and I will refresh you.
Matthew 11:28

God so loved the world, that he gave his only-begotten Son, to the end that all that believe in him should not perish, but have everlasting life. *John 3:16*

This is a true saying, and worthy of all men to be received, that Christ Jesus came into the world to save sinners. *1 Timothy 1:15*

If any man sin, we have an Advocate with the Father, Jesus Christ the righteous; and he is the perfect offering for our sins, and not for ours only, but for the sins of the whole world. *1 John 2:1-2*

The Peace

All stand. The Celebrant says to the people

The peace of the Lord be always with you.

People And with thy spirit.

Then the Ministers and People may greet one another in the name of the Lord.

The Holy Communion

The Offertory

The Great Thanksgiving

Eucharistic Prayer I

The people remain standing.

Celebrant The Lord be with you.

People And with thy spirit.

Celebrant Lift up your hearts.

People We lift them up unto the Lord.

Celebrant Let us give thanks unto our Lord God.

People It is meet and right so to do.

Then, facing the Holy Table, the Celebrant proceeds

It is very meet, right, and our bounden duty, that we should at all times, and in all places, give thanks unto thee, O Lord, holy Father, almighty, everlasting God.

Here a Proper Preface is sung or said on all Sundays, and on other occasions as appointed.

Therefore with Angels and Archangels, and with all the company of heaven, we laud and magnify thy glorious Name; evermore praising thee, and saying,

Celebrant and People

Holy, holy, holy, Lord God of Hosts: Heaven and earth are full of thy glory. Glory be to thee, O Lord Most High.

Here may be added

Blessed is he that cometh in the name of the Lord. Hosanna in the highest.

The people kneel or stand.

Then the Celebrant continues

All glory be to thee, Almighty God, our heavenly Father, for that thou, of thy tender mercy, didst give thine only Son Jesus Christ to suffer death upon the cross for our redemption; who made there, by his one oblation of himself once offered, a full perfect, and sufficient sacrifice, oblation, and satisfaction, for the sins of the whole world; and did institute, and in his holy Gospel command us to continue, a perpetual memory of that his precious death and sacrifice, until his coming again.

For in the night in which he was betrayed, he took bread; and when he had given thanks, he brake it, and gave it to his disciples, saying, "Take, eat, this is my Body, which is given for you. Do this in remembrance of me."

Likewise, after supper, he took the cup; and when he had given thanks, he gave it to them, saying, "Drink ye all of this; for this is my Blood of the New Testament, which is shed for you, and for many, for the remission of sins. Do this, as oft as ye shall drink it, in remembrance of me."

Wherefore, O Lord and heavenly Father, according to the institution of thy dearly beloved Son our Savior Jesus Christ, we, thy humble servants, do celebrate and make here before thy divine Majesty, with these thy holy gifts, which we now offer unto thee, the memorial thy Son hath commanded us to make; having in remembrance his blessed passion and precious death, his mighty resurrection and glorious ascension; rendering unto thee most hearty thanks for the innumerable benefits procured unto us by the same.

And we most humbly beseech thee, O merciful Father, to hear us; and, of thy almighty goodness, vouchsafe to bless and sanctify, with thy Word and Holy Spirit, these thy gifts and creatures of bread and wine; that we, receiving them according to thy Son our Savior Jesus Christ's holy institution, in remembrance of his death and passion, may be partakers of his most blessed Body and Blood.

And we earnestly desire thy fatherly goodness mercifully to accept this our sacrifice of praise and thanksgiving; most humbly beseeching thee to grant that, by the merits and death of thy Son Jesus Christ, and through faith in his blood, we, and all thy whole Church, may obtain remission of our sins, and all other benefits of his passion

And here we offer and present unto thee, O Lord, our selves, our souls and bodies, to be a reasonable, holy, and living sacrifice unto thee; humbly beseeching thee that we, and all others who shall be partakers of this Holy Communion, may worthily receive the most precious Body and Blood of thy Son Jesus Christ, be filled with thy grace and heavenly benediction, and made one body with him, that he may dwell in us, and we in him.

And although we are unworthy, through our manifold sins, to offer unto thee any sacrifice, yet we beseech thee to accept this our bounden duty and service, not weighing our merits, but pardoning our offenses, through Jesus Christ our Lord;

By whom, and with whom, in the unity of the Holy Ghost, all honor and glory be unto thee, O Father Almighty, world without end. *AMEN.*

And now, as our Savior Christ hath taught us, we are bold to say,

People and Celebrant

Our Father, who art in heaven, hallowed be thy Name, thy kingdom come, thy will be done, on earth as it is in heaven. Give us this day our daily bread. And forgive us our trespasses, as we forgive those who trespass against us. And lead us not into temptation, but deliver us from evil. For thine is the kingdom, and the power, and the glory, for ever and ever. Amen.

The Breaking of the Bread

The Celebrant breaks the consecrated Bread.

A period of silence is kept.

Then may be sung or said

[Alleluia.] Christ our Passover is sacrificed for us; *Therefore let us keep the feast. [Alleluia.]*

The following or some other suitable anthem may be sung or said here

O Lamb of God, that takest away the sins of the world, have mercy upon us. O Lamb of God, that takest away the sins of the world, have mercy upon us. O Lamb of God, that takest away the sins of the world, grant us thy peace.

The following prayer may be said. The People may join in saying this prayer

We do not presume to come to this thy Table, O merciful Lord, trusting in our own righteousness, but in thy manifold and great mercies. We are not worthy so much as to gather up the crumbs under thy Table. But thou art the same Lord whose property is always to have mercy. Grant us therefore, gracious Lord, so to eat the flesh of thy dear Son Jesus Christ, and to drink his blood, that we may evermore dwell in him, and he in us. *Amen.*

Facing the people, the Celebrant may say the following Invitation

The Gifts of God for the People of God.

and may add Take them in remembrance that Christ died for you, and feed on him in your hearts by faith, with thanksgiving.

The Bread and the Cup are given to the communicants with these words

The Body of our Lord Jesus Christ, which was given for thee, preserve thy body and soul unto everlasting life. Take and eat this in remembrance that Christ died for thee, and feed on him in thy heart by faith, with thanksgiving.

The Blood of our Lord Jesus Christ, which was shed for thee, preserve thy body and soul unto everlasting life. Drink this in remembrance that Christ's Blood was shed for thee, and be thankful.

or with these words

The Body (Blood) of our Lord Jesus Christ keep you in everlasting life. *[Amen.]*

or with these words

The Body of Christ, the bread of heaven. *[Amen.]*
The Blood of Christ, the cup of salvation. *[Amen.]*

After Communion, the Celebrant says

Let us pray.

The People may join in saying this prayer

Almighty and everliving God, we most heartily thank thee for that thou dost feed us, in these holy mysteries with the spiritual food of the most precious Body and Blood of thy Son our Savior Jesus Christ; and dost assure us thereby of thy favor and goodness towards us; and that we are very members incorporate in the mystical body of thy Son, the blessed company of all faithful people; and are also heirs, through hope, of thy everlasting kingdom. And we humbly beseech thee, O heavenly Father, so to assist us with thy grace, that we may continue in that holy fellowship, and do all such good works as thou hast prepared for us to walk in; through Jesus Christ our Lord, to whom, with thee and the Holy Ghost, be all honor and glory, world without end. *Amen.*

The Bishop when present, or the Priest, gives the blessing

The peace of God, which passeth all understanding, keep your hearts and minds in the knowledge and love of God, and of his Son Jesus Christ our Lord; and the blessing of God Almighty, the Father, the Son, and the Holy Ghost, be amongst you, and remain with you always. *Amen.*

or this

The blessing of God Almighty, the Father, the Son, and the Holy Spirit, be upon you and remain with you for ever. *Amen.*

The Deacon, or the Celebrant, may dismiss the people with these words

	Let us go forth in the name of Christ.
People	Thanks be to God.

or this

Deacon	Go in peace to love and serve the Lord.
People	Thanks be to God.

or the following

Deacon Let us go forth into the world, rejoining in the power of the Spirit.

People Thanks be to God.

or this

Deacon Let us bless the Lord.

People Thanks be to God.

A Penitential Order: Rite Two

For use at the beginning of the Liturgy, or as a *separate service.*

The people standing, the Celebrant says

Blessed be God: Father, Son, and Holy Spirit.

People And blessed be his kingdom, now and for ever. Amen.

In place of the above, from Easter Day through the Day of Pentecost

Celebrant Alleluia. Christ is risen.
People The Lord is risen indeed. Alleluia.

In Lent and on other penitential occasions

Celebrant Bless the Lord who forgives all our sins;
People His mercy endures for ever.

The Decalogue may be said, the people kneeling

The Celebrant may read an introductory sentence

Jesus said, "The first commandment is this: Hear, O Israel: The Lord our God is the only Lord. Love the Lord your God with all your heart, with all your soul, with all your mind, and with all your strength. The second is this: Love your neighbor as yourself. There is no other commandment greater than these." *Mark 12:29-31*

The Deacon or Celebrant then says

Let us confess our sins against God and our neighbor.

Silence may be kept.

Minister and People

Most merciful God, we confess that we have sinned against you in thought, word, and deed, by what we have done, and by what we have left undone. We have not loved you with our whole heart; we have not loved our neighbors as ourselves. We are truly sorry and we humbly repent. For the sake of your Son Jesus Christ, have mercy on us and forgive us; that we may delight in your will, and walk in your ways, to the glory of your Name. Amen.

The Bishop when present, or the Priest, stands and says

Almighty God have mercy on you, forgive you all your sins through our Lord Jesus Christ, strengthen you in all goodness, and by the power of the Holy Spirit keep you eternal life. *Amen.*

When this Order is used at the beginning of the Liturgy, the service continues with the Kyrie eleison, the Trisagion, or the Gloria in excelsis.

When used separately, it concludes with suitable prayers, and the Grace or a blessing.

The Holy Eucharist
Rite Two

The Word of God

The people standing, the Celebrant says

Blessed be God: Father, Son, and Holy Spirit.

People And blessed be his kingdom, now and for ever. Amen.

In place of the above, from Easter Day through the Day of Pentecost

Celebrant Alleluia. Christ is risen.

People The Lord is risen indeed. Alleluia.

In Lent and on other penitential occasions

Celebrant Bless the Lord who forgives all our sins;

People His mercy endures for ever.

The Celebrant may say

Almighty God, to you all hearts are open, all desires known, and from you no secrets are hid: Cleanse the thoughts of our hearts by the inspiration of your Holy Spirit, that we may perfectly love you, and worthily magnify your holy Name; through Christ our Lord. *Amen.*

When appointed, the following hymn or some other song of praise is sung or said, all standing

Glory to God in the highest, and peace to his people on earth.

Lord God, heavenly King, almighty God and Father, we worship you, we give you thanks, we praise you for your glory.

Lord Jesus Christ, only Son of the Father, Lord God, Lamb of God, you take away the sin of the world: have mercy on us; you are seated at the right hand of the Father: receive our prayer.

For you alone are the Holy One, you alone are the Lord, you alone are the Most High, Jesus Christ, with the Holy Spirit, in the glory of God the Father. Amen.

On other occasions the following is used

Lord, have mercy. *Christ, have mercy.* Lord, have mercy.

or this

Kyrie eleison. *Christe eleison.* Kyrie eleison.

or this

Holy God, Holy and Mighty, Holy Immortal One, *Have mercy upon us.*

The Collect of the Day

The Celebrant says to the people

The Lord be with you.

People And also with you.

Celebrant Let us pray.

The Celebrant says the Collect.

People Amen.

The Lessons

The people sit. One or two Lessons, as appointed, are read, the Reader first saying

A Reading (Lesson) from ___________.

After each Reading, the Reader may say

The Word of the Lord.

People Thanks be to God.

Silence may follow.

A Psalm, hymn, or anthem may follow each Reading.

Then, all standing, the Deacon or a Priest reads the Gospel, first saying

The Holy Gospel of our Lord Jesus Christ according to ____________.

People Glory to you, Lord Christ.

After the Gospel, the Reader says

The Gospel of the Lord.

People Praise to you, Lord Christ.

The Sermon

On Sundays and other Major Feasts there follows, all standing

The Nicene Creed

We believe in one God, the Father, the Almighty, maker of heaven and earth, of all that is, seen and unseen.

We believe in one Lord, Jesus Christ, the only

Son of God, eternally begotten of the Father, God from God, Light from Light, true God from true God, begotten, not made, of one Being with the Father. Through him all things were made. For us and for our salvation he came down from heaven: by the power of the Holy Spirit he became incarnate from the Virgin Mary, and was made man. For our sake he was crucified under Pontius Pilate; he suffered death and was buried. On the third day he rose again in accordance with the Scriptures; he ascended into heaven and is seated at the right hand of the Father. He will come again in glory to judge the living and the dead, and his kingdom will have no end.

We believe in the Holy Spirit, the Lord, the giver of life, who proceeds from the Father and the Son. With the Father and the Son he is worshiped and glorified. He has spoken through the Prophets. We believe in one holy catholic and apostolic Church. We acknowl-. edge one baptism for the forgiveness of sins. We look for the resurrection of the dead, and the life of the world to come. Amen.

The Prayers of the People

Prayer is offered with intercession using the following or other forms or authorized prayers

Form III

The Leader and People pray responsively

Father, we pray for your holy Catholic Church; *That we all may be one.*

Grant that every member of the Church may truly and humbly serve you; *That your Name may be glorified by all people.*

We pray for all bishops, priests, and deacons; *That they may be faithful ministers of your Word and Sacraments.*

We pray for all who govern and hold authority in the nations of the world; *That there may be justice and peace on the earth.*

Give us grace to do your will in all that we undertake *That our works may find favor in your sight.*

Have compassion on those who suffer from any grief or trouble; *That they may be delivered from their distress.*

Give to the departed eternal rest; *Let light perpetual shine upon them.*

We praise you for your saints who have entered into joy; *May we also come to share in your heavenly kingdom.*

Let us pray for our own needs and those of others.

Silence

The People may add their own petitions.

The Celebrant adds a concluding Collect.

Form VI

The Leader and People pray responsively

In peace, we pray to you, Lord God.

Silence

For all people in their daily life and work; *For our families, friends, and neighbors, and for those who are alone.*

For this community, the nation, and the world; *For all who work for justice, freedom, and peace.*

For the just and proper use of your creation; *For the victims of hunger, fear, injustice, and oppression.*

For all who are in danger, sorrow, or any kind of trouble; *For those who minister to the sick, the friendless, and the needy.*

For the peace and unity of the Church of God; *For all who proclaim the Gospel, and all who seek the Truth.*

For *[N.* our Presiding Bishop, and *N.* (N.) our Bishop(s); and for] all bishops and other ministers; *For all who serve God in his Church.*

For the special needs and concerns of this congregation.

Silence

The People may add their own petitions

Hear us, Lord; *For your mercy is great.*

We thank you, Lord, for all the blessings of this life.

Silence

The People may add their own thanksgivings

We will exalt you, O God our King; *And praise your Name for ever and ever.*

We pray for all who have died, that they may have a place in your eternal kingdom.

Silence

The People may add their own petitions

Lord, let your loving-kindness be upon them; *Who put their trust in you.*

We pray to you also for the forgiveness of our sins.

Silence may be kept.

Leader and People

Have mercy upon us, most merciful Father; in your compassion forgive us our sins, known and unknown, things done and left undone; and so uphold us by your Spirit that we may live and serve you in newness of life, to the honor and glory of your Name; through Jesus Christ our Lord. Amen.

The Celebrant concludes with an absolution or a *suitable Collect.*

Confession of Sin

The Deacon or *Celebrant may say*

Let us confess our sins against God and our neighbor.

Silence may be kept.

Minister and People

Most merciful God, we confess that we have sinned against you in thought, word, and deed, by what we have done, and by what we have left undone. We have not loved you with our whole heart; we have not loved our neighbors as ourselves. We are truly sorry and we humbly repent. For the sake of your Son Jesus Christ, have mercy on us and forgive us; that we may delight in your will, and walk in your ways, to the glory of your Name. Amen.

The Bishop when present, or the Priest, stands and says

Almighty God have mercy on you, forgive you all your sins through our Lord Jesus Christ, strengthen you in all goodness, and by the power of the Holy Spirit keep you in eternal life. *Amen.*

The Peace

All stand. The Celebrant says to the people

The peace of the Lord .be always with you.

People And also with you.

Then the Ministers and People may greet one another in the name of the Lord.

The Holy Communion

The Offertory

The Great Thanksgiving

Eucharistic Prayer A

The people remain standing.

The Lord be with you.

People And also with you.

Celebrant Lift up your hearts.

People We lift them to the Lord.

Celebrant Let us give thanks to the Lord our God.

People It is right to give him thanks and praise.

Then, facing the Holy Table, the Celebrant proceeds

It is right, and a good and joyful thing, always and everywhere to give thanks to you, Father Almighty, Creator of heaven and earth.

Here a Proper Preface is sung or said on all Sundays, and on other occasions as appointed.

Therefore we praise you, joining our voices with Angels and Archangels and with all the company of heaven, who for ever sing this hymn to proclaim the glory of your Name:

Celebrant and People

Holy, holy, holy Lord, God of power and might, heaven and earth are full of your glory. Hosanna in the highest. Blessed is he who comes in the name of the Lord. Hosanna in the highest.

The people stand or kneel.

Then the Celebrant continues

Holy and gracious Father: In your infinite love you made us for yourself; and, when we had fallen into sin and become subject to evil and death, you, in your mercy, sent Jesus Christ, your only and eternal Son, to share our human nature, to live and die as one of us, to reconcile us to you, the God and Father of all.

He stretched out his arms upon the cross, and offered himself, in obedience to your will, a perfect sacrifice for the whole world.

On the night he was handed over to suffering and death, our Lord Jesus Christ took bread; and when he had given thanks to you, he broke it, and gave it to his disciples, and said, "Take, eat: This is my Body, which is given for you. Do this for the remembrance of me."

After supper he took the cup of wine; and when he had given thanks, he gave it to them, and said, "Drink this, all of you: This is my Blood of the new Covenant, which is shed for you and for many for the forgiveness of sins. Whenever you drink it, do this for the remembrance of me."

Therefore we proclaim the mystery of faith:

Celebrant and People

Christ has died. Christ is risen. Christ will come again.

The Celebrant continues

We celebrate the memorial of our redemption, O Father, in this sacrifice of praise and thanksgiving. Recalling his death, resurrection, and ascension, we offer you these gifts.

Sanctify them by your Holy Spirit to be for your people the Body and Blood of your Son, the holy food and drink of new and unending life in him. Sanctify us also that we may faithfully receive this holy Sacrament, and serve you in unity, constancy, and peace; and at the last day bring us with all your saints into the joy of your eternal kingdom.

All this we ask through your Son Jesus Christ. By him, and with him, and in him, in the unity of the Holy Spirit all honor and glory is yours, Almighty Father, now and for ever. *AMEN.*

As our Savior Christ has taught us, we now pray,

Our Father in heaven, hallowed be your Name, your kingdom come, your will be done, on earth as in heaven. Give us today our daily bread. Forgive us our sins as we forgive those who sin against us. Save us from the time of trial and deliver us from evil. For the kingdom, the power, and the glory are yours, now and for ever. Amen.

The Breaking of the Bread

A period of silence is kept while the Celebrant breaks the consecrated bread.

Then may be sung or said

[Alleluia.] Christ our Passover is sacrificed for us; *Therefore let us keep the feast. [Alleluia.]*

In place of, or in addition to, the preceding, some other suitable anthem may be used.

Facing the people, the Celebrant says the following Invitation

The Gifts of God for the People of God.

and may add Take them in remembrance that Christ died for you, and feed on him in your hearts by faith, with thanksgiving.

The Bread and the Cup are given to the communicants with the following words

The Body (Blood) of our Lord Jesus Christ keep you in everlasting life. *[Amen.]*

or with these words

The Body of Christ, the bread of heaven. *[Amen.]* The Blood of Christ, the cup of salvation. *[Amen.]*

During the ministration of Communion, hymns, psalms, or anthems may be sung.

After Communion, the Celebrant says

Let us pray.

Celebrant and People

Eternal God, heavenly Father, you have graciously accepted us as living members of your Son our Savior Jesus Christ, and you have fed us with spiritual food in the Sacrament of his Body and Blood. Send us now into the world in peace, and grant us strength and courage to love and serve you with gladness and singleness of heart; through Christ our Lord. Amen.

The Bishop when present, or the Priest, may bless the people.

The Deacon, or the Celebrant, dismisses them with these words

Let us go forth in the name of Christ.
People Thanks be to God.

or this

Deacon Go in peace to love and serve the Lord.
People Thanks be to God.

or this

Deacon Let us go forth into the world, rejoicing in the power of the Spirit.
People Thanks be to God.

or this

Deacon Let us bless the Lord.
People Thanks be to God.

Communion under Special Circumstances

The Celebrant, whether priest or deacon, reads a passage of Scripture appropriate to the day or occasion, or else one of the following

God so loved the world that he gave his only Son, that whoever believes in him should not perish, but have eternal life. *John 3:16*

Jesus said, "I am the bread of life; whoever comes to me shall not hunger, and whoever believes in me shall never thirst." *John 6:35*

Jesus said, "I am the living bread which came down from heaven; if anyone eats of this bread, he will live for ever; and the bread which I shall give for the life of the world is my flesh. For my flesh is food indeed, and my blood is drink indeed. Whoever eats my flesh and drinks my blood abides in me, and I in him." *John 6:51,55-56*

Jesus said, "Abide in me, as I in you. As the branch cannot bear fruit by itself, unless it abides in the vine, neither can you, unless you abide in me. I am the vine, you are the branches. By this my Father is glorified, that you bear much fruit, and so prove to be my disciples. As the Father has loved me; so have I loved you; abide in my love."
John 15:4-5a,8-9

Suitable prayers may be offered.

Almighty Father, whose dear Son, on the night before he suffered, instituted the Sacrament of his Body and Blood: Mercifully grant that we may receive it thankfully in remembrance of Jesus Christ our Lord, who in these holy mysteries gives us a pledge of eternal life; and who lives and reigns for ever and ever. *Amen.*

A Confession of Sin may follow.

Most merciful God, we confess that we have sinned against you in thought, word, and deed, by what we have done, and by what we have left undone. We have not loved you with our whole heart; we have not loved our neighbors as ourselves. We are truly sorry and we humbly repent. For the sake of your Son Jesus Christ, have mercy on us and forgive us; that we may delight in your will, and walk in your ways, to the glory of your Name. Amen.

The Priest alone says

Almighty God have mercy on you, forgive you all your sins through our Lord Jesus Christ, strengthen you in all goodness, and by the power of the Holy Spirit keep you in eternal life. *Amen.*

The Peace may then be exchanged.

The Lord's Prayer is said, the Celebrant first saying

Let us pray in the words our Savior Christ has taught us.

Our Father, who art in heaven, hallowed be thy Name, thy kingdom come, thy will be done,. on earth as it is in heaven. Give us this day our daily bread. And forgive us our trespasses, as we forgive those who trespass against us. And lead us not into temptation, but deliver us from evil. For thine is the kingdom, and the power, and the glory, for ever and ever. Amen.

The Celebrant may say the following Invitation

The Gifts of God for the People of God.

and may add Take them in remembrance that Christ died for you, and feed on him in your hearts by faith, with thanksgiving.

The Sacrament is administered with the following or other words

The Body (Blood) of our Lord Jesus Christ keep you in everlasting life. *[Amen.]*

One of the usual postcommunion prayers is then said, or the following

Gracious Father, we give you praise and thanks for this Holy Communion of the Body and Blood of your beloved Son Jesus Christ, the pledge of our redemption; and we pray that it may bring us forgiveness of our sins, strength in our weakness, and everlasting salvation; through Jesus Christ our Lord. *Amen.*

The service concludes with a blessing or with a dismissal

Let us bless the Lord. *Thanks be to God.*

The Reconciliation of a Penitent

Form One

The Penitent begins

Bless me, for I have sinned.

The Priest says

The Lord be in your heart and upon your lips that you may truly and humbly confess your sins: In the Name of the Father, and of the Son, and of the Holy Spirit. *Amen.*

Penitent

I confess to Almighty God, to his Church, and to you, that I have sinned by my own fault in thought, word, and deed, in things done and left undone; especially ___________. For these and all other sins which I cannot now remember, I am truly sorry. I pray God to have mercy on me. I firmly intend amendment of life, and I humbly beg forgiveness of God and his Church, and ask you for counsel, direction, and absolution.

Here the Priest may offer counsel, direction, and comfort.

The Priest then pronounces this absolution

Our Lord Jesus Christ, who has left power to his Church to absolve all sinners who truly repent and believe in him, of his great mercy forgive you all your offenses; and by his authority committed to me, I absolve you from all your sins: In the Name of the Father, and of the Son, and of the Holy Spirit. *Amen.*

or this

Our Lord Jesus Christ, who offered himself to

be sacrificed for us to the Father, and who conferred power on his Church to forgive sins, absolve you through my ministry by the grace of the Holy Spirit, and restore you in the perfect peace of the Church. *Amen.*

The Priest adds

The Lord has put away all your sins.

Penitent Thanks be to God.

The Priest concludes

Go *(or* abide) in peace, and pray for me, a sinner.

Declaration of Forgiveness to be used by a Deacon or Lay Person

Our Lord Jesus Christ, who offered himself to be sacrificed for us to the Father, forgives your sins by the grace of the Holy Spirit. *Amen.*

Form Two

The Priest and Penitent begin as follows

Have mercy on me, O God, according to your loving-kindness; in your great compassion blot out my offenses. Wash me through and through from my wickedness, and cleanse me from my sin. For I know my transgressions only too well, and my sin is ever before me.

Holy God, Holy and Mighty, Holy Immortal One, have mercy upon us.

Penitent Pray for me, a sinner.

Priest May God in his love enlighten your heart, that you may remember in truth all your sins and his unfailing mercy. *Amen.*

Appropriate verses of Scripture may be said. The Priest then continues

Now, in the presence of Christ, and of me, his

minister, confess your sins with a humble and obedient heart to Almighty God, our Creator and our Redeemer.

The Penitent says

Holy God, heavenly Father, you formed me from the dust in your image and likeness, and redeemed me from sin and death by the cross of your Son Jesus Christ. Through the water of baptism you clothed me with the shining garment of his righteousness, and established me among your children in your kingdom. But I have squandered the inheritance of your saints, and have wandered far in a land that is waste.

Especially, I confess to you and to the Church . . . *Here the penitent confesses particular sins.*

Therefore, O Lord, from these and all other sins I cannot now remember, I turn to you in sorrow and repentance. Receive me again into the arms of your mercy, and restore me to the blessed company of your faithful people; through him in whom you have redeemed the world, your Son our Savior Jesus Christ. Amen.

The Priest may then offer words of comfort and counsel.

Priest

Will you turn again to Christ as your Lord?

Penitent I will.

Priest

Do you, then, forgive those who have sinned against you?

Penitent I forgive them.

Priest

May Almighty God in mercy receive your confession of sorrow and of faith, strengthen you in all goodness, and by the power of the Holy Spirit keep you in eternal life. *Amen.*

The Priest then lays a hand upon the penitent's head (or extends a hand over the penitent), saying one of the following

Our Lord Jesus Christ, who offered himself to be sacrificed for us to the Father, and who conferred power on his Church to forgive sins, absolve you through my ministry by the grace of the Holy Spirit, and restore you in the perfect peace of the Church. *Amen:*

or this

Our Lord Jesus Christ, who has left power to his Church to absolve all sinners who truly repent and believe in him, of his great mercy forgive you all your offenses; and by his authority committed to me, I absolve you from all your sins: In the Name of the Father, and of the Son, and of the Holy Spirit. *Amen.*

The Priest concludes

Now there is rejoicing in heaven; for you were lost, and are found; you were dead, and are now alive in Christ Jesus our Lord. Go *(or* abide) in peace; The Lord has put away all your sins.

Penitent Thanks be to God.

Declaration of Forgiveness to be used by a Deacon or Lay Person

Our Lord Jesus Christ, who offered himself to be sacrificed for us to the Father, forgives your sins by the grace of the Holy Spirit. *Amen.*

Ministration to the Sick

In case of illness, the Minister of the Congregation is to be notified.

The Celebrant begins the service with the following or some other greeting

Peace be to this house (place), and to all who dwell in it.

Part I. Ministry of the Word

One or more of the following or other passages of Scripture are read

General

Blessed be the God and Father of our Lord Jesus Christ, the Father of mercies and God of all comfort, who comforts us in all our affliction, so that we may be able to comfort those who are in any affliction, with the comfort with which we ourselves are comforted by God. For as we share abundantly in Christ's sufferings, so through Christ we share abundantly in comfort too. *2 Corinthians l:3-5*

Penitence

[And getting into a boat Jesus crossed over and came to his own city.] And behold, they brought to him a paralytic, lying on his bed; and when Jesus saw their faith he said to the paralytic, "Take heart, my son; your sins are forgiven." And behold, some of the scribes said to themselves, "This man is blaspheming." But Jesus, knowing their thoughts, said, "Why do you think evil in your hearts? For which is easier, to say, 'Your sins are forgiven,' or to say, 'Rise and walk'? But that you may know that the Son of man has authority on earth to forgive sins" – he then said to the paralytic – "Rise, take up your bed and go home." Arid he rose and went home. When the crowds saw it, they were afraid, and they glorified God, who had given such authority to men. *Matthew 9:2-8*

When Anointing is to follow

Is any among you sick? Let him call for the elders of the church, and let them pray over him, anointing him with oil in the name of the Lord; and the prayer of faith will save the sick man, and the Lord will raise him up; and if he has committed sins, he will be forgiven. Therefore confess your sins to one another, and pray for one another, that you may be healed. The prayer of a righteous man has great power in its effects. *James 5:14-16*

Prayers may be offered according to the occasion.

A general confession may be said

Most merciful God, we confess that we have sinned against you in thought, word, and deed, by what we have done, and by what we have left undone. We have not loved you with our whole heart; we have not loved our neighbors as ourselves. We are truly sorry and we humbly repent. For the sake of your Son Jesus Christ, have mercy on us and forgive us; that we may delight in your will, and walk in your ways, to the glory of your Name. Amen.

The Priest alone says

Almighty God have mercy on you, forgive you all your sins through our Lord Jesus Christ, strengthen you in all goodness, and by the power of the Holy Spirit keep you in eternal life. *Amen.*

Part II. Laying on of Hands and Anointing

Oil may be blessed by the Priest.

The following anthem is said

Savior of the world, by your cross and precious blood you have redeemed us; *Save us, and help us, we humbly beseech you, O Lord.*

The Priest then lays hands upon the sick person, and says one of the following

N., I lay my hands upon you in the Name of the Father, and of the Son, and of the Holy Spirit, beseeching our Lord Jesus Christ to sustain you with his presence, to drive away all sickness of body and spirit, and to give you that victory of life and peace which will enable you to serve him both now and evermore. *Amen.*

or the following

N., I lay my hands upon you in the Name of our Lord and Savior Jesus Christ, beseeching him to uphold you and fill you with his grace, that you may know the healing power of his love. *Amen.*

If the person is to be anointed, the Priest dips a thumb in the holy oil, and makes the sign of the cross on the sick person's forehead, saying

N., I anoint you with oil in the Name of the Father, and of the Son, and of the Holy Spirit. *Amen.*

The Priest may add

As you are outwardly anointed with this holy oil, so may our heavenly Father grant you the inward anointing of the Holy Spirit. Of his great mercy, may he forgive you your sins, release you from suffering, and restore you to wholeness and strength. May he deliver you from all evil, preserve you in all goodness, and bring you to everlasting life; through Jesus Christ our Lord. *Amen.*

In cases of necessity, a deacon or lay person may perform the anointing, using oil blessed by a bishop or priest.

If Communion is not to follow, the Lord's Prayer is now said.

The Priest concludes

The Almighty Lord, who is a strong tower to all who put their trust in him, to whom all things in heaven, on earth, and under the earth bow and obey: Be now and evermore your defense, and make you know and feel that the only Name under heaven given for health and salvation is the Name of our Lord Jesus Christ. *Amen.*

Part III. Holy Communion

Communion Under Special Circumstances, page

107. If a person desires to receive the Sacrament, but, by reason of extreme sickness or physical disability, is unable to eat and drink the Bread and Wine, the Celebrant is to assure that person that all the benefits of Communion are received, even though the Sacrament is not received with the mouth.

Prayers for the Sick

For a Sick Person

O Father of mercies and God of all comfort, our only help in time of need: We humbly beseech thee to behold, visit, and relieve thy sick servant *N.* for whom our prayers are desired. Look upon *him* with the eyes of thy mercy; comfort *him* with a sense of thy goodness; preserve *him* from the temptations of the enemy; and give *him* patience under *his* affliction. In thy good time, restore *him* to health, and enable *him* to lead the residue of *his* life in thy fear, and to thy glory; and grant that finally *he* may dwell with thee in life everlasting; through Jesus Christ our Lord. *Amen.*

For Recovery from Sickness

O God, the strength of the weak and the comfort of sufferers: Mercifully accept our prayers, and grant to your servant *N.* the help of your power, that *his* sickness may be turned into health, and our sorrow into joy; through Jesus Christ our Lord. *Amen.*

or this

O God of heavenly powers, by the might of your command you drive away from our bodies all sickness and all infirmity: Be present in your goodness with your servant *N.*, that *his* weakness may be banished and *his* strength restored; and that, *his* health being renewed, *he* may bless your holy Name; through Jesus Christ our Lord. *Amen.*

For a Sick Child

Heavenly Father, watch with us over your child *N.,* and grant that *he* may be restored to that perfect health which it is yours alone to give; through Jesus Christ our Lord. *Amen.*

or this

Lord Jesus Christ, Good Shepherd of the sheep, you gather the lambs in your arms and carry them in your bosom: We commend to your loving care this child *N.* Relieve *his* pain, guard *him* from all danger, restore to *him* your gifts of gladness and strength, and raise *him* up to a life of service to you. Hear us, we pray, for your dear Name's sake. *Amen.*

Before an Operation

Almighty God our heavenly Father, graciously comfort your servant *N.* in *his* suffering, and bless the means made use of for *his* cure. Fill *his* heart with confidence that, though at times *he* may be afraid, *he* yet may put *his* trust in you; through Jesus Christ our Lord. *Amen.*

or this

Strengthen your servant *N., O* God, to do what *he* has to do and bear what *he* has to bear; that, accepting your healing gifts through the skill of surgeons and nurses, *he* may be restored to usefulness in your world with a thankful heart; through Jesus Christ our Lord. *Amen.*

For Strength and Confidence

Heavenly Father, giver of life and health: Comfort and relieve your sick servant *N.,* and give your power of healing to those who minister to *his* needs, that *he* may be strengthened in *his* weakness and have confidence in your loving care; through Jesus Christ our Lord. *Amen.*

For the Sanctification of Illness

Sanctify, O Lord, the sickness of your servant *N.*, that the sense of *his* weakness may add strength to *his* faith and seriousness to *his* repentance; and grant that *he* may live with you in everlasting life; through Jesus Christ our Lord. *Amen.*

For Health of Body and Soul

May God the Father bless you, God the Son heal you, God the Holy Spirit give you strength. May God the holy and undivided Trinity guard your body, save your soul, and bring you safely to his heavenly country; where he lives and reigns for ever and ever. *Amen.*

For Doctors and Nurses

Sanctify, O Lord, those whom you have called to the study and practice of the arts of healing, and to the prevention of disease and pain. Strengthen them by your life-giving Spirit, that by their ministries the health of the community may be promoted and your creation glorified; through Jesus Christ our Lord. *Amen.*

Thanksgiving for a Beginning of Recovery

O Lord, your compassions never fail and your mercies are new every morning: We give you thanks for giving our brother (sister) *N* both relief from pain and hope of health renewed. Continue in *him,* we pray, the good work you have begun; that *he,* daily increasing in bodily strength, and rejoicing in your goodness, may so order *his* life and conduct that *he* may always think and do those things that please you; through Jesus Christ our Lord. *Amen.*

Prayers for use by a Sick Person

For Trust in God

O God, the source of all health: So fill my heart with faith in your love, that with calm expectancy I may make room for your power to possess me, and gracefully accept your healing; through Jesus Christ our Lord. *Amen.*

In Pain

Lord Jesus Christ, by your patience in suffering you hallowed earthly pain and gave us the example of obedience to your Father's will: Be near me in my time of weakness and pain; sustain me by your grace, that my strength and courage may not fail; heal me according to your will; and help me always to believe that what happens to me here is of little account if you hold me in eternal life, my Lord and my God. *Amen.*

For Sleep

O heavenly Father, you give your children sleep for the refreshing of soul and body: Grant me this gift, I pray; keep me in that perfect peace which you have promised to those whose minds are fixed on you; and give me such a sense of your presence, that in the hours of silence I may enjoy the blessed assurance of your love; through Jesus Christ our Savior. *Amen.*

In the Morning

This is another day, O Lord. I know not what it will bring forth, but make me ready, Lord, for whatever it may be. If I am to stand up, help me to stand bravely. If I am to sit still, help me to sit quietly. If I am to lie low, help me. to do it patiently. And if I am to do nothing, let me do it gallantly. Make these words more than words, and give me the Spirit of Jesus. *Amen.*

Ministration at the Time of Death

When a person is near death, the Minister of the Congregation should -be notified, in order that the ministrations of the Church may be provided.

A Prayer for a Person near Death

Almighty God, look on this your servant, lying in great weakness, and comfort *him* with the promise of life everlasting, given in the resurrection of your Son Jesus Christ our Lord. *Amen.*

Litany at the Time of Death

When possible, it is desirable that members of the family and friends come together to join in the Utany.

God the Father, *Have mercy on your servant.*

God the Son, *Have mercy on your servant.*

God the Holy Spirit, *Have mercy on your servant.*

Holy Trinity, one God, *Have mercy on your servant.*

From all evil, from all sin, from all tribulation, *Good Lord, deliver* him.

By your holy Incarnation, by your Cross and Passion, by your precious Death and Burial, *Good Lord, deliver* him.

By your glorious Resurrection and Ascension, and by the Coming of the Holy Spirit, *Good Lord, deliver* him.

We sinners beseech you to hear us, Lord Christ: That it may please you to deliver the soul of your servant from the power of evil, and from eternal death, *We beseech you to hear us, good Lord.*

That it may please you mercifully to pardon all *his* sins. *We beseech you to hear us, good Lord.*

That it may please you to grant *him* a place of refreshment and everlasting blessedness, *We beseech you to hear us, good Lord.*

That it may please you to give *him* joy and gladness in your kingdom, with your saints in light, *We beseech you to hear us, good Lord.*

Jesus, Lamb of God: *Have mercy on* him.

Jesus, bearer of our sins: *Have mercy on* him.

Jesus, redeemer of the world: *Give* him *your peace.*

Lord, have mercy. *Christ, have mercy.* Lord, have mercy.

Officiant and People

Our Father, who art in heaven, hallowed be

thy Name, thy kingdom come, thy will be done, on earth as it is in heaven. Give us this day our daily bread. And forgive us our trespasses, as we forgive those who trespass against us. And lead us not into temptation, but deliver us from evil.

The Officiant says this Collect

Let us pray.

Deliver your servant, *N., O* Sovereign Lord Christ, from all evil, and set *him* free from every bond; that *he* may rest with all your saints in the eternal habitations; where with the Father and the Holy Spirit you live and reign, one God, for ever and ever. *Amen.*

A Commendation at the Time of Death

Depart, O Christian soul, out of this world; In the name of God the Father Almighty who created you; In the name of Jesus Christ who redeemed you; In the name of the Holy Spirit who sanctifies you. May your rest be this day in peace, and your dwelling place in the Paradise of God.

A Commendatory Prayer

Into your hands, O merciful Savior, we commend your servant *N.* Acknowledge, we humbly beseech you, a sheep of your own fold, a lamb of your own flock, a sinner of your own redeeming. Receive *him* into the arms of your mercy, into the blessed rest of everlasting peace, and into the glorious company of the saints in light. *Amen.*

May *his* soul and the souls of all the departed, through the mercy of God, rest in peace. *Amen.*

Prayers for a Vigil

It is appropriate that the family and friends come

together for prayers prior to the funeral. Suitable Psalms, Lessons, and Collects (such as those in the Burial service) may be used. The Litany at the Time of Death may be said, or the following

Dear Friends: It was our Lord Jesus himself who said, "Come to me, all 'you who labor and are burdened, and I will give you rest." Let us pray, then, for our brother (sister) *N.*, that *he* may rest from *his* labors, and enter into the light of God's eternal sabbath rest.

Receive, O Lord, your servant, for *he* returns to you. *Into your hands, O Lord, we* com-*mend our brother (sister) N.*

Wash *him* in the holy font of everlasting life, and clothe *him* in *his* heavenly wedding garment. *Into your hands, O Lord, we commend our brother (sister) N.*

May *he* hear your. words of invitation, "Come, you blessed of my Father." *Into your hands, O Lord, we commend our brother (sister) N.*

May *he* gaze upon you, Lord, face to face, and taste the blessedness of perfect rest. *Into your hands, O Lord, we commend our brother (sister) N.*

May angels surround *him,* and saints welcome *him* in peace. *Into your hands, O Lord, we commend our brother (sister) N.*

The Officiant concludes

Almighty God, our Father in heaven, before whom live all who die in the Lord: Receive our *brother N.* into the courts of your heavenly dwelling place. Let *his* heart and soul now ring out in joy to you, O Lord, the living God, and the God of those who live. This we ask through Christ our Lord. *Amen.*

Burial of the Dead

1. *The body is received. The celebrant may meet the body and conduct it into the church or chapel, or it may be in place before the congregation assembles.*

2. *Anthems from Holy Scripture or psalms may be sung or said, or a hymn may be sung.*

3. *Prayer may be offered for the bereaved.*

4. *One or more passages of Holy Scripture are read. Psalms, hymns, or anthems may follow the readings. If there is to be a Communion, the last Reading is from the Gospel.*

5. *A homily may follow the Readings; and the Apostles' Creed may be recited.*

6. *Prayer, including the Lord's Prayer, is offered,* as *follows:*

The Prayers

For our brother (sister) *N.,* let us pray to our Lord Jesus Christ who said, "I am Resurrection and I am Life."

Lord, you consoled Martha and Mary in their distress; draw near to us who mourn for *N.,* and dry the tears of those who weep. *Hear us, Lord.*

You wept at the grave of Lazarus, your friend; comfort us in our sorrow. *Hear us, Lord.*

You raised the dead to life; give to our brother (sister) eternal life. *Hear us, Lord.*

You promised paradise to the thief who repented; bring our brother (sister) to the joys of heaven. *Hear us, Lord.*

Our brother (sister) was washed in Baptism and anointed with the Holy Spirit; give *him* fellowship with all your saints. *Hear us, Lord.*

He was nourished with your Body and Blood; grant *him* a place at the table in your heavenly kingdom. *Hear us, Lord.*

Comfort us in our sorrows at the death of our brother (sister); let our faith be our consolation, and eternal life our hope.

Silence may be kept.

The Celebrant concludes with one of the following or some other prayer.

Lord Jesus Christ, we commend to you our brother (sister) *N.,* who was reborn by water and the Spirit in Holy Baptism. Grant that *his* death may recall to us your victory over death, and be an occasion for us to renew our trust in your Father's love. Give us, we pray, the faith to follow where you have led the way; and where you live and reign with the Father and the Holy Spirit, to the ages of ages. *Amen.*

or the following

Father of all, we pray to you for N., and for all those whom we love but see no longer. Grant to them eternal rest. Let light perpetual shine upon them. May his soul and the souls of all the departed, through the mercy of God, rest in peace. Amen.

The Commendation

The Celebrant and other ministers take their places at the body.

Give rest, O Christ, to your servant(s) with your saints, where sorrow and pain are no more, neither sighing, but life everlasting.

You only are immortal, the creator and maker of mankind; and we are mortal, formed of the earth, and to earth shall we return. For so did you ordain when you created me, saying, "You are dust, and to dust you shall return." All of us go down to the dust; yet even at the grave we make our song: Alleluia, alleluia, alleluia.

Give rest, O Christ, to your servant(s) with your saints, where sorrow and pain are no more, neither sighing, but life everlasting.

The Celebrant, facing the body, says

Into your hands, O merciful Savior, we commend your servant *N.* Acknowledge, we humbly beseech you, a sheep of your own fold, a lamb of your own flock, a sinner of your own redeeming. Receive *him* into the arms of your mercy, into the blessed rest of everlasting peace, and into the glorious company of the saints in light. *Amen.*

The Celebrant, or the Bishop if present, may then bless the people, and a Deacon or other Minister may dismiss them, saying

Let us go forth in the name of Christ. *Thanks be to God.*

Additional Prayers

Almighty God, with whom still live the spirits of those who die in the Lord, and with whom the souls of the faithful are in joy and felicity: We give you heartfelt thanks for the good examples of all your servants, who, having finished their course in faith, now find rest and refreshment. May we, with all who have died in the true faith of your holy Name, have perfect fulfillment and bliss in your eternal and everlasting glory, through Jesus Christ our Lord. *Amen.*

O God, whose days are without end, and whose mercies cannot be numbered: Make us, we pray, deeply aware of the shortness and uncertainty of human life; and let your Holy Spirit lead us in holiness and righteousness all our days; that, when we shall have served ·you in our generation, we may be gathered to our ancestors, having the testimony of a good conscience, in the communion of the Catholic Church, in the confidence of a certain faith, in the comfort of a religious and holy hope, in favor with you, our God, and in perfect charity with the world. All this we ask through Jesus Christ our Lord. *Amen.*

O God; the King of saints, we praise and glorify your holy Name for all your servants who have finished their course in your faith and fear: for the blessed Virgin Mary; for the holy patriarchs, prophets, apostles, and martyrs; and for all your other righteous servants, known to us and unknown; and we pray that, encouraged by their examples, aided by their prayers, and strengthened by their fellowship, we also may be partakers of the inheritance of the saints in light; through the merits of your Son Jesus Christ our Lord. *Amen.*

Lord Jesus Christ, by your death you took away the sting of death: Grant to us your servants so to follow in faith where you have led the way, that we may at length fall asleep peacefully in you and wake up in your likeness; for your tender mercies' sake. *Amen.*

Father of all, we pray to you for those we love, but see no longer: Grant them your peace; let light perpetual shine upon them; and, in your loving wisdom and almighty power, work in them the good purpose of your perfect will; through Jesus Christ our Lord. *Amen.*

Merciful God, Father of our Lord Jesus Christ who is the Resurrection and the Life: Raise us, we humbly pray, from the death of sin to the life of righteousness; that when we depart this life we may rest in him, and at the resurrection receive that blessing which your well-beloved Son shall then pronounce: "Come, you blessed of my Father, receive the kingdom prepared for you from the beginning of the world." Grant this, O merciful Father, through Jesus Christ, our Mediator and Redeemer. *Amen.*

Grant, O Lord, to all who are bereaved the spirit of faith and courage, that they may have strength to meet the days to come with steadfastness and patience; not sorrowing as those without hope, but in thankful remembrance of your great goodness, and in the joyful expectation of eternal life with those they love. And this we ask in the Name of Jesus Christ our Savior. *Amen.*

Almighty God, Father of mercies and giver of comfort: Deal graciously, we pray, with all who mourn; that, casting all their care on you, they may know the consolation of your love; through Jesus Christ our Lord. *Amen.*

The Psalter

1

1. Happy are they who have not walked in the counsel of the wicked, * nor lingered in the way of sinners, nor sat in the seats of the scornful!

2. Their delight is in the law of the LORD, * and they meditate on his law day and night.

3. They are like trees planted by streams of water, bearing fruit in due season, with leaves that do not wither; * everything they do shall prosper.

4. It is not so with the wicked; * they are like chaff which the wind blows away.

5. Therefore the wicked shall not stand up-
right when judgment comes, * nor the sinner in
the council of the righteous.
6. For the LORD knows the way of the righteous, *but the way of the wicked is doomed.

22 *(1-21)*

1. My God, my God, why have you for-
saken me? * and are so far from my cry and
from the words of my distress?
2. O my God, I cry in the daytime, but you do
not answer; * by night as well, but I find no rest.
3. Yet you are the Holy One, * enthroned
upon the praises of Israel.
4. Our forefathers put their trust in you; *
they trusted, and you delivered them.
5. They cried out to you and were delivered;

* they trusted in you and were not put to shame.

6. But as for me, I am a worm and no man, * scorned by all and despised by the people.

7. All who see me laugh me to scorn; * they curl their lips and wag their heads, saying,

8. "He trusted in the LORD, let him deliver him; * let him rescue him, if he delights in him."

9. Yet you are he who took me out of the womb, * and kept me safe upon my mother's breast.

10. I have been entrusted to you ever since I was born; * you were my God when I was still in my mother's womb.

11. Be not far from me, for trouble is near, * and there is none to help.

12. Many young bulls encircle me;* strong bulls of Bashan surround me.

13. They open wide their jaws at me, * like a ravening and a roaring lion.

14. I am poured out like water; all my bones are out of joint; * my heart within my breast is melting wax.

15. My mouth is dried out like a pot-sherd; my tongue sticks to the roof of my mouth; * and you have laid me in the dust of the grave.

16. Packs of dogs close me in, and gangs of evildoers circle around me; * they pierce my hands and my feet; I can count all my bones.

17. They stare and gloat over me;* they divide my garments among them; they cast lots for my clothing.

18. Be not far away, O LORD; * you are my strength; hasten to help me.

19. Save me from the sword, * my life from the power of the dog.

20. Save me from the lion's mouth, * my wretched body from the horns of wild bulls.

21. I will declare your Name to my brethren; * in the midst of the congregation I will praise you.

23 *King James Version*

1. The LORD is my shepherd; * I shall not want.

2. He maketh me to lie down in green pastures;* he leadeth me beside the still waters.

3. He restoreth my soul; * he leadeth me in the paths of righteousness for his Name's sake.

4. Yea, though I walk through the valley of the shadow of death, I will fear no evil; * for thou art with me; thy rod and thy staff, they comfort me.

5. Thou preparest a table before me in the
presence of mine enemies; * thou anointest
my head with oil; my cup runneth over.

6. Surely goodness and mercy shall follow
me all the days of my life, *and I will dwell in
the house of the LORD for ever.

27

1. The LORD is my light and my salvation;
whom then shall I fear? * the LORD is the
strength of my life; of whom then shall I be
afraid?

2. When evildoers came upon me to eat up
my flesh, * it was they, my foes and my adversaries, who stumbled and fell.

3. Though an army should encamp against
me,* yet my heart shall not be afraid;

4. And though war should rise up against
me, * yet will I put my trust in him.

5. One thing have I asked of the LORD; one thing I seek; * that I may dwell in the house of the LORD all the days of my life;

6. To behold the fair beauty of the LORD * and to seek him in his temple.

7. For in the day of trouble he shall keep me safe in his shelter; * he shall hide me in the secrecy of his dwelling and set me high upon a rock.

8. Even now he lifts up my head * above my enemies round about me.

9. Therefore I will offer in his dwelling an oblation with sounds of great gladness; * I will sing and make music to the LORD.

10. Hearken to my voice, O LORD, when I call; * have mercy on me and answer me.

11. You speak in my heart and say, "Seek my face."* Your face, LORD, will I seek.

12. Hide not your face from me, * nor turn away your servant in displeasure.

13. You have been my helper; cast me not away; * do not forsake me, O God of my salvation.

14. Though my father and my mother forsake me, * the LORD will sustain me.

15. Show me your way, O LORD;* lead me on a level path, because of my enemies.

16. Deliver me not into the hand of my adversaries, * for false witnesses have risen up against me, and also those who speak malice.

17. What if I had not believed that I should see the goodness of the LORD * in the land of the living!

18. O tarry and await the LORD'S pleasure; be strong, and he shall comfort your heart; * wait patiently for the LORD.

46

1. God is our refuge and strength, * a very present help in trouble.

2. Therefore we will not fear, though the earth be moved, * and though the mountains be toppled into the depths of the sea;

3. Though its waters rage and foam, * and though the mountains tremble at its tumult.

4. The LORD of hosts is with us; * the God of Jacob is our stronghold.

5. There is a river whose streams make glad the city of God, * the holy habitation of the Most High.

6. God is in the midst of her; she shall not be overthrown'; * God shall help her at the break of day.

7. The nations make much ado, and the kingdoms are shaken; * God has spoken, and the earth shall melt away.

8. The LORD of hosts is with us; * the God of Jacob is our stronghold.

9. Come now and look upon the works of the LORD, * what awesome things he has done on earth.

10. It is he who makes war to cease in all the world; * he breaks the bow, and shatters the spear, and burns the shields with fire.

11. "Be still, then, and know that I am God; * I will be exalted among the nations; I will be exalted in the earth."

12. The LORD of hosts is with us; * the God of Jacob is our stronghold.

91

1. He who dwells in the shelter of the Most High, * abides under the shadow of the Almighty.

2. He shall say to the LORD, "You are my refuge and my stronghold, * my God in whom I put my trust."

3. He shall deliver you from the snare of the hunter * and from the deadly pestilence.

4. He shall cover you with his pinions, and you shall find refuge under his wings; * his faithfulness shall be a shield and buckler.

5. You shall not be afraid of any terror by night, * nor of the arrow that flies by day;

6. Of the plague that stalks in the darkness, * nor of the sickness that lays waste at mid-day.

7. A thousand shall fall at your side and ten thousand at your right hand, * but it shall not come near you.

8. Your eyes have only to behold * to see the reward of the wicked.

9. Because you have made the LORD your refuge, * and the Most High your habitation,

10. There shall no evil happen to you, * neither shall any plague come near your dwelling.

11. For he shall give his angels charge over you,* to keep you in all your ways.

12. They shall bear you in their hands, * lest you dash your foot against a stone.

13. You shall tread upon the lion and adder; * you shall trample the young lion and the serpent under your feet.

14. Because he is bound to me in love, therefore will I deliver him; * I will protect him, because he knows my Name.

15. He shall call upon me, and I will answer him; * I am with him in trouble; I will rescue him and bring him to honor.

16. With long life will I satisfy 'him, * and show him my salvation.

98

1. Sing to the LORD a new song, * for he has done marvelous things.

2. With his right hand and his holy arm * has he won for himself the victory.

3. The LORD has made known his victory; * his righteousness has he openly shown in the sight of the nations.

4. He remembers his mercy and faithfulness to the house of Israel, * and all the ends of the earth have seen the victory of our God.

5. Shout with joy to the LORD, all you lands; * lift up your voice, rejoice, and sing.

6. Sing to the LORD with the harp,* with the harp and the voice of song.

7. With trumpets and the sound of the horn * shout with joy before the King, the LORD.

8. Let the sea make a noise and all that is in it, * the lands and those who dwell therein.

9. Let the rivers clap their hands, * and let the hills ring out with joy before the LORD, when he comes to judge the earth.

10. In righteousness shall he judge the world * and the peoples with equity.

100

1. Be joyful in the LORD, all you lands; * serve the LORD with gladness and come before his presence with a song.

2. Know this: The LORD himself is God; * he himself has made us, and we are his; we are his people and the sheep of his pasture.

3. Enter his gates with thanksgiving; go into his courts with praise; * give thanks to him and call upon his Name.

4. For the LORD is good; his mercy is everlasting; * and his faithfulness endures from age to age.

103

1. Bless the LORD, O my soul, * and all that is within me, bless his holy Name.

2. Bless the LORD, O my soul, * and forget not all his benefits.

3. He forgives all your sins * and heals all your infirmities;

4. He redeems your life from the grave * and crowns you with mercy and loving-kindness;

5. He satisfies you with good things, * and your youth is renewed like an eagle's.

6. The LORD executes righteousness * and judgment for all who are oppressed.

7. He made his ways known to Moses * and his works to the children of Israel.

8. The LORD is full of compassion and mercy, * slow to anger and of great kindness.

9. He will not always accuse us, * nor will he keep his anger for ever.

10. He has not dealt with us according to our sins, * nor rewarded us according to our wickedness.

11. For as the heavens are high above the earth, * so is his mercy great upon those who fear him.

12. As far as the east is from the west, * so far has he removed our sins from us.

13. As a father cares for his children, * so does the LORD care for those who fear him.

14. For he himself knows whereof we are made; * he remembers that we are but dust.

15. Our days are like the grass; * we flourish like a flower of the field;

16. When the wind goes over it, it is gone,* and its place shall know it no more.

17. But the merciful goodness of the LORD endures for ever on those who fear him, * and his righteousness on children's children;

18. On those who keep his covenant * and remember his commandments and do them.

19. The LORD has set his throne in heaven, * and his kingship has dominion over all.

20. Bless the LORD, you angels of his, you mighty ones who do his bidding, * and hearken to the voice of his word.

21. Bless the LORD, all you his hosts, * you ministers of his who do his will.

22. Bless the LORD, all you works of his, in all places of his dominion; * bless the LORD, O my soul.

121

1. I lift up my eyes to the hills;* from where is my help to come?

2. My help comes from. the LORD, * the maker of heaven and earth.

3. He will not let your foot be *moved* * and he.who watches *over* you will not fall asleep.

4. Behold, he who keeps watch *over* Israel * shall neither slumber nor sleep;

5. The LORD himself watches *over* you; * the LORD is your shade at your right hand.

6. So that the sun shall not strike you by day, * nor the moon by night.

7. The LORD shall preserve you from all evil; * it is he who shall keep you safe.

8. The LORD shall watch *over* your going out and your coming in, * from this time forth for *evermore.*

122

1. I was glad when they said to me, * "Let us go to the house of the LORD."

2. Now our feet are standing * within your gates, O Jerusalem.

3. Jerusalem is built as a city * that is at unity with itself;

4. To which the tribes go up, the tribes of the LORD, * the assembly of Israel, to praise the Name of the LORD.

5. For there are the thrones of judgment, * the thrones of the house of David.

6. Pray for the peace of Jerusalem: * "May they prosper who love you.

7. Peace be within your walls, * and quietness within your towers.

8. For my breathren and companions' sake, * I pray for your prosperity.

9. Because of the house of the LORD our God, * I will seek to do you good."

138

1. I will give thank? to you, O LORD, with my whole heart; * before the gods I will sing your
praise.

2. I will bow down toward your holy temple and praise your Name, * because of your love and faithfulness;

3. For you have glorified your Name * and your word above all things.

4. When I called, you answered me; * you increased my strength within me.

5. All the kings of the earth will praise you, O LORD, * when they have heard the words of your mouth.

6. They will sing of the ways of the LORD, * that great is the glory of the LORD.

7. Though the LORD be high, he cares for the lowly; * he perceives the haughty from afar.

8. Though I walk in the midst of trouble, you keep me safe; * you stretch forth your hand against the fury of my enemies; your right hand shall save me.

9. The LORD will make good his purpose for me;* O LORD, your love endures for ever; do not abandon the works of your hands.

146

1. Hallelujah! Praise the LORD, O my soul! * I will praise the LORD as long as I live; I will sing praises to my God while I have my being.

2. Put not your trust in rulers, nor in any child of earth, * for there is no help in them.

3. When they breathe their last, they return to earth, * and in that day their thoughts perish.

4. Happy are they who have the God of Jacob for their help * whose hope is in the LORD their God;

5. Who made heaven and earth, the seas, and all that is in them; * who keeps his promise for ever;

6. Who gives justice to those who are oppressed, * and food to those who hunger.

7. The LORD sets the prisoners free; the LORD opens the eyes of the blind;* the LORD lifts up those who are bowed down;

8. The LORD loves the righteous; the LORD cares for the stranger; * he sustains the orphan and widow, but frustrates the way of the wicked.

9. The LORD shall reign for ever, * your God, O Zion, throughout all generations. Hallelujah!

Prayers and Thanksgivings

Prayers for the World

2. *For All Sorts and Conditions of Men*

O God, the creator and preserver of all mankind, we humbly beseech thee for all sorts and conditions of men; that thou wouldest be pleased to make thy ways known unto them, thy saving health unto all nations. More especially we pray for thy holy Church universal; that it may be so guided and governed by thy good spirit, that all who profess and call themselves Christians may be led into the way of truth, and hold the faith in unity of spirit, in the bond of peace, and in righteousness of life. Finally, we commend to thy fatherly goodness all those who are in any ways afflicted or distressed, in mind, body, or estate; [especially those for whom our prayers are desired]; that it may please thee to comfort and relieve them according to their several necessities, giving them patience under their sufferings, and a happy issue out of all their afflictions. And this we beg for Jesus Christ's sake. *Amen.*

5. For Peace Among the Nations

Almighty God our heavenly Father, guide the nations of the world into the way of justice and truth, and establish among them that peace which is the fruit of righteousness, that they may become the kingdom of our Lord and Savior Jesus Christ. *Amen.*

Prayers for the Church

9. For Clergy and People

Almighty and everlasting God, from whom cometh every good and perfect gift: Send down upon our bishops, and other clergy, and upon the congregations committed to their charge, the healthful Spirit of thy grace; and, that they may truly please thee, pour upon them the continual dew of thy blessing. Grant this, O Lord, for the honor of our Advocate and Mediator, Jesus Christ. *Amen.*

11. For the Parish

Almighty and everliving God, ruler of all things in heaven and earth, hear our prayers for this parish family. Strengthen the- faithful, arouse the careless, and restore the penitent. Grant us all things necessary for our common life, and bring us all to be of one heart and mind within your holy Church; through Jesus Christ our Lord. *Amen.*

Prayer for National Life

18. For our Country

Almighty God, who hast given us this good land for our heritage: We humbly beseech thee that we may always prove ourselves a people mindful of thy favor and glad to do thy will. Bless our land with honorable industry, sound learning, and pure manners. Save us from violence, discord, and confusion; from pride and arrogance, and from every evil way. Defend our liberties, and fashion into one united people the multitudes brought hither out of many kindreds and tongues. Endue with the spirit of wisdom those to whom in thy Name we entrust the authority of government, that there may be justice and peace at home, and that, through obedience to thy law, we may show forth thy praise among the nations of the earth. In the time of prosperity, fill our hearts with thankfulness, and in the day of trouble, suffer not our trust in thee to fail; all which we ask through Jesus Christ our Lord. *Amen.*

Prayers for Family and Personal Life

45. For Families

Almighty God, our heavenly Father, who settest the solitary in families: We commend to thy continual care the homes in which thy people dwell. Put far from them, we beseech thee, every root of bitterness, the desire of vainglory, and the pride of life. Fill them with faith, virtue, knowledge, temperance, patience, godliness. Knit together in constant af- fection those who, in holy wedlock, have been made one flesh. Turn the hearts of the parents to the children, and the hearts of the children to the parents; and so enkindle fervent charity among us all, that we may evermore be kindly affectioned one to another; through Jesus Christ our Lord. *Amen.*

47. For Young Persons

God our Father, you see your children growing up in an unsteady and confusing world: Show them that your ways give more life than the ways of the world, and that following you is better than chasing after selfish goals. Help them to take failure, not as a measure of their worth, but as a chance for a new start. Give them strength to hold their faith in you, and to keep alive their joy in your creation; through Jesus Christ our Lord. *Amen.*

48. For Those Who Live Alone

Almighty God, whose Son had nowhere to lay his head: Grant that those who live alone may not be lonely in their solitude, but that, following in his steps, they may find fulfillment in loving you and their neighbors; through Jesus Christ our Lord. *Amen.*

49. *For the Aged*

Look with mercy, O God our Father, on all whose increasing years bring them weakness, distress, or isolation. Provide for them homes of dignity and peace; give them understanding helpers, and the willingness to accept help; and, as their strength diminishes, increase their faith and their assurance of your love. This we ask in the name of Jesus Christ our Lord. *Amen.*

54. *For those we Love*

Almighty God, we entrust all who are dear to us to *thy* never-failing care and love, for this life and the life to come, knowing that *thou art* doing for them better things than we can desire or pray for; through Jesus Christ our Lord. *Amen.*

59. *For Quiet Confidence*

O God of peace, *who hast* taught us that in

returning and rest we shall be saved, in quietness and in confidence shall be our strength: By the might of *thy* Spirit lift us, we pray *thee,* to *thy* presence, where we may be still and know that *thou art* God; through Jesus Christ our Lord. *Amen.*

62. A Prayer attributed to St. Francis

Lord, make us instruments of your peace. Where there is hatred, let us sow love; where there is injury, pardon; where there is discord, union; where there is doubt, faith; where there is despair, hope; where there is darkness, light; where there is sadness, joy. Grant that we may not so much seek to be consoled as to console; to be understood as to understand; to be loved as to love. For it is in giving that we receive; it is in pardoning that we are pardoned; and it is in dying that we are born to eternal life. *Amen.*

Other Prayers

70. Grace at Meals

Give us grateful hearts, our Father, for all *thy* mercies, and make us mindful of the needs of others; through Jesus Christ our Lord. *Amen.*

or this

Bless, O Lord, *thy* gifts to our use and us to *thy* service; for Christ's sake. *Amen.*

or this

Blessed are you, O Lord God, King of the Universe, for you give us food to sustain our lives and make our hearts glad; through Jesus Christ our Lord. *Amen.*

or this

For these and all his mercies, God's holy Name be blessed and praised; through Jesus Christ our Lord. *Amen.*